Published by CelebrityPress®, Orlando, FL

CelebrityPress® is a registered trademark

Printed in the United States of America.

ISBN: 978-0-9895187-0-3
LCCN: 2013941450

Most CelebrityPress® titles are available at special quantity discounts for bulk purchases for sales promotions, premiums, fundraising, and educational use. Special versions or book excerpts can also be created to fit specific needs.

For more information, please write:

CelebrityPress®
520 N. Orlando Ave, #2
Winter Park, FL 32789
or call 1.877.261.4930

Visit us online at www.CelebrityPressPublishing.com

CELEBRITY PRESS®
Winter Park, Florida

CONTENTS

FOREWORD

Within these pages, you'll read about clients who have been coached by some of the best fitness coaches in the industry, along with the exact programs they used to achieve the incredible results you'll read about. All of the coaches included in this book are part of an elite group of fitness professionals, the Results Fitness University Mastermind Coaching Group.

You'll notice that the programs in this book all follow the same principles, working off of the same basic template, but designed individually for each client and with each of the coach's expertise in their niche.

Each program has been designed for the client after taking them through a thorough screening called The Functional Movement Screen.

What you can expect from each program is a scientifically-designed, thought out plan that will include a version of our Results Fitness dynamic RAMP warm up. Ramp stands for Range of motion, Activation, Movement Preparation. With the warm up, you'll get your body warmed up and ready for that work out. From there, you'll see core exercises, which will include core stability along with power development exercises in most programs. Power is one of the first qualities we lose as we age, and should be included as part of your fitness program. From there, you'll notice these programs include the basic movements of the human body, including squatting, bending, pushing, pulling, balancing, lunging and twisting. Strengthening your body in all of these movements, staying in balance will lead to the most effective results and a decreased risk of injuries.

As you read the stories of the clients in this book, we hope you are inspired to start your own fitness program. By giving you the exact programs we used to help these clients achieve their results, you'll have an idea of what it will take for you to do the same. There are clients of all different backgrounds, ages, training histories and goals…you're bound to find someone who resonates with you.

In addition, be sure to check out where the coaches are from, and if you're lucky, you'll be able to visit one of their gyms and have your own program designed specifically for you and your goals!

This group of fitness coaches is changing the way fitness is done and you'll see that in their programs.

CHAPTER 1

WORKING OUT THROUGH PREGNANCY AND BEYOND

BY RACHEL & ALWYN COSGROVE*
& THE RESULTS FITNESS TEAM
(program designed by the RF team)

Jeanette Yamamoto started at Results Fitness after having her first baby, determined to get her body back. "I started with the intention to lose the excess weight I had gained from my first pregnancy – 2 years earlier!!"

It only took her 12 weeks to shed the weight she had gained with her first pregnancy. "I was able to shed my pregnancy weight and be in the best shape I had been in YEARS, with the intention to continue my weight loss goals."

Then along came baby number two. "I was pregnant again. With my second pregnancy, I was determined to continue with my training as long as possible, and have a healthier go at it the second time around. I continued workouts 3-4 times a week and was blessed enough during my pregnancy to be able to workout until the day before giving birth to my son."

"Afterwards, I took my required 6 weeks off from the gym, and then came back on a mission to get my sexy self back!!"

"I have worked diligently to drop my fat percent from 32% to 22% and fit back into my size 8 clothes - now with room to spare! I am a true believer in the Results Fitness philosophies and will continue to abide by them for the rest of my life!!"

Below is the exact program Jeanette Yamamoto used immediately following her second pregnancy to kick start her come back to her sexy self. Below is what she did for 8 weeks which includes two phases. Each phase is four weeks and includes two strength programs.

PHASE 1

Warm Up –
Perform one set of each for 8-10 reps each as your warm up before starting the program each day.

Foam Roll

Brettzel

½ Kneeling hip flexor w/ thoracic extension

Walking Knee Hugs

Backwards walking Inverted Hamstring

Walking Lunge with Rotation

Walking Heel to Butt

Walking Cross Behind Lunge

In Place Spidermans

Deep Squat 3

PHASE ONE DAY ONE STRENGTH PROGRAM

EXERCISE	SETS	REPS	TEMPO	REST
Corrective Exercise/Rehab				
Passive Lock Single Leg Bridge	1-2	5 ea	151	0
Wall Slides	1-2	10	Slow	60s
Core Training				
A1 Stiff Arm Pulldowns	1-2	12	222	0
A2 Tall Kneeling Anti Rotation Press	1-2	3 ea	1-15-1	60
Resistance Exercise				
B1 Straddle Squat	2-3	12	Mod	60
B2 3 Point DB Row	2-3	12 ea	Mod	60
C1 Step Up	2-3	12 ea	Mod	60
C2 Incline SA DB Bench Press	2-3	12 ea	Mod	60
D1 SHELC	2-3	12	Slow	60
D2 High to Low	2-3	12	Mod	60
Cable Rows				
Finisher				
Air Dyne Intervals	1	2-4	60	120

PHASE ONE DAY TWO STRENGTH PROGRAM

EXERCISE	SETS	REPS	TEMPO	REST
Corrective Exercise				
Passive Lock Single Leg Bridge	1-2	5 ea	151	0
Wall Slides	1-2	10	Slow	60s
Core Training				
A1 Passive Single Leg Lowering	1-2	10 ea	Slow	0
A2 ½ Kneeling cable bar chops	1-2	10 ea	Slow	60
Resistance Training				
B1 Supine Lateral Ball Roll	2-3	6 ea	212	60
B2 Overhead Press	2-3	12	Mod	60
C1 Static Lunge	2-3	12 ea	Mod	60
C2 Kneeling CG Pulldown	2-3	12	Mod	60
D1 Single Leg Shoulder Elevated Hip Bridge on 12" plyo	2-3	12 ea	Slow	60
D2 Push Ups	2-3	12	Mod	60
Finisher				
Air Dyne Intervals	1	2-4	60	120

PHASE 2

Warm Up –

Perform the following exercises for 8-10 reps for 1 set each before performing the Phase two strength workouts.

Foam Roll

Brettzel

Quadruped w/ thoracic ext/rot

Walking Cross Body Knee Hugs

Walking Reverse Lunge with turn and reach

Crawling Spider Mans

Walking Lateral Lunges

Squat to Stand

PHASE TWO DAY ONE STRENGTH PROGRAM

EXERCISE	SETS	REPS	TEMPO	REST
Corrective Exercise/Prehab				
Active Lock Single Leg Bridge	1-2	5 ea	151	0
Prone Ys & Ts	1-2	12 ea	Slow	0
Core Training				
A1 Front Plank	2-3	1	30-45s	45s
Resistance Training				
B1 Bulgarian Split Squat	3-4	8 ea	Mod	0
B2 TRX Inverted Rows	3-4	8	Mod	0
B3 Romanian Deadlift	3-4	8	Mod	90
C1 T- Push Ups	3-4	4 ea	Mod	0
C2 Val Slide Reverse Lunge	3-4	8ea	Mod	60
Finisher				
Air Dyne Intervals	1	5-6	30	60

PHASE TWO DAY TWO STRENGTH PROGRAM

EXERCISE	SETS	REPS	TEMPO	REST
Corrective Exercise				
Active Lock Single Leg Bridge	1-2	5 ea	151	0
Prone Y's & T's	1-2	12 ea	Slow	0
Core Training				
A1 Tall Kneeling Cable Bar Lifts	2	10 ea	Slow	60
Resistance Training				
B1 Front Squat	3-4	8	Mod	0
B2 Single Arm Push Press	3-4	8 ea	Fast	0
B3 SHELC	3-4	8	Mod	0
C1 Kneeling WG Pulldown	3-4	8	Mod	0
C2 Single Arm Loaded Dynamic Lunge	3-4	8 ea	Norm	60
Finisher				
Air Dyne Intervals	1	5-6	30	60

Alwyn & Rachel Cosgrove own Results Fitness located in Southern California which is one of the top ten gyms in the United States by Men's Health Magazine and named one of the Best Gyms by Women's Health Magazine. Going on their 14th year of business they also coach other fitness coaches who are modeling their business after theirs. Included in this book are some of their affiliate fitness business owners. Together they are on a mission to change the way fitness is done. To learn more about Results Fitness visit: www.results-fitness.com and www. resultsfitnessuniversity.com.

About Alwyn

Born in Scotland and initially exposed to fitness training through an intense competitive sport martial arts background, Alwyn Cosgrove began reading and studying any training-related material he could get his hands on. This led Alwyn to formal academic studies in Sports Performance at West Lothian College and then progressed on to receiving an honors degree in Sports Science from Chester College, the University of Liverpool.

During his career as a fitness coach, Alwyn began with assisting in martial arts lessons in 1986 and teaching fitness classes in 1989. He has studied under all of the top fitness professionals and coaches in the world and has worked with a wide variety of clientele, from general population clientele to several top-level athletes, World Champions and professionals in a multitude of sports.

A sought after 'expert' for several of the country's leading publications including being a regular contributor to *Men's Health* magazine, Alwyn has co-authored three books in the *"New Rules of Lifting"* series and currently spends his time training clients, training his staff at Results Fitness, speaking on the lecture circuit and coaching fitness trainers worldwide in their businesses.

For the past decade, with his wife Rachel, Alwyn runs Results Fitness in Santa Clarita,

California – which has been three times named one of America's Top Gyms by *Men's Health* magazine, a gym that specializes in programs for real-world busy people, and prides itself on "changing the way fitness is done – period!"

About Rachel

Rachel Cosgrove is the best selling author of *The Female Body Breakthrough* (published by Rodale November 2009), and is a fitness professional who specializes in getting women of all ages into the best shape of their lives. She owns and operates Results Fitness with her husband in southern California. She has a BS in Exercise Physiology and earned her CSCS from the National Strength and Conditioning Association. She has competed in fitness competitions, is an Ironman triathlete and has set a powerlifting record. She has her own column in *Women's Health Magazine* and has also been featured in *More Magazine, Real Simple, Muscle and Fitness Hers, Shape Magazine, Fitness Magazine, Men's Health, Men's Fitness* and *Oxygen*. She has also had TV appearances on Fox, ABC and WGN. She is on a mission to help as many women make a breakthrough as she can.

For more information on Rachel visit her websites at: www.rachelcosgrove. com and www.thefemalebodybreakthrough.com.

CHAPTER 2

EVERY BODY NEEDS A TUNE UP

BY AMY WUNSCH, MSPT

Grab three of your closest friends and pack up your car because you, my friend, are going on a road trip! This trip will be the stuff of legends, people will tell its stories for years to come. You have snacks, your GPS and what you are SURE is the greatest mix of music ever made. You turn your key expecting to hear the rev of the engine, but you are met with a "click, click, click." DANG. You try again, "click," and then silence. The trip is over before it starts. Did you forget to fill the tank? Did you leave the lights on all night? What happened?

Your body is your vehicle to get through life. You can't expect to get very far on a 1/2 a tank of gas and an old battery, just like you can't expect to reach your goals without proper body maintenance. Like your car, your body needs general and continuous maintenance to make sure it is running well enough to do the tasks you demand from it.

How much maintenance your body needs depends on its current condition and what you want to be able to do with it. You may be an athlete who has a lot of "use wear" on the body. This person is going 80 miles per hour at all times and slams their brakes. They demand a lot from their body, which can wear it

23

out quickly. It seems obvious that this person would benefit from some maintenance, but what about the people on the other end of the spectrum?

The couch potato will suffer from "disuse wear" requiring just as much body work as anyone else, if not more. Let me explain. I bought my first car from my grandma. It was a 1988 Chevy Corsica and it was awesome. Much to my surprise all four tires blew in the first 6 months. No, I am not a spectacularly untalented driver. My grandma hadn't driven that car in a long while, causing soft spots on the tires. I had demanded more out of my car than my tires were able to give me. This same phenomenon happens with the human body. When we don't use it, it weakens and sets us up to blow our "tires" which render the vehicle useless.

Imagine how well you would take care of your car if you only got one to use for your entire life. You do only get one body in your lifetime. It will last longer the better you take care of it. For this reason, we at Results Fitness have developed the Tune Up class. Just like general maintenance for your car, the Tune Up class keeps your vehicle (your body) moving and prepared to handle what lies in the road ahead.

The Tune Up program is the 4-point inspection for your body. It addresses flexibility, alignment, mobility and stability (FAMS). Your ability to coordinate and control these factors dictates how well and how long your body will perform. What does this mean? Lets get back to our road trip.

Flexibility and Mobility: When your joints don't move well, and your muscles don't stretch, it is like driving your car with the parking brake on. It takes a lot more effort to get from point A to point B and it will only move the expense of your brake pads and tires. In the case of your body, your tires and brake pads are your muscles and joints.

Alignment: Poor body alignment is like driving your car on a spare tire (or donut). A donut is smaller and less sturdy than the other 3 tires. Driving on a donut only allows you to go 50 MPH (taking you longer to get to your destination) and if driven on long enough will wear out the rest of your car.

Stability is your ability to time and sequence muscle contractions to keep the body balanced and erect. Stability issues are like driving your car on ice; you may hit the brake and slow down, but then again you may hit the brake and skid out of control. This is an unpredictable situation that can be detrimental to your performance and safety.

In short, if you lack flexibility, mobility, alignment or stability you will waste energy, take longer to reach your goals, experience a decline in performance and be predisposed to injury. What good is reaching your destination if you can't use your body when you get there? Remember, your body is your ONE vehicle in life and a Tune Up program will help you take care of it.

I realize that taking care of your body may not sound "sexy" or "fun" to most people. I don't expect people to get excited like I do when they see a perfect dead-lift. I do, however, surmise that everyone could get at least mildly worked up over feeling better, looking better, being able to do fun activities without pain, or having a more fulfilling sex life. Do I have your attention?

GETTING THERE: THE "BLOCK TOWER VS. PYRAMID" THEORY

As a kid, I loved building things. I wanted to see how high I could get my block tower. Like most kids (SQUIRREL!), my attention span was limited. I wanted to build my tower as high as I possibly could in a hurry. I would build straight up balancing one block on another, reaching heights of a whopping one foot off the ground...that is, until the blocks tumbled to the floor. Then, I started to get smart. I began to build my tower like a pyramid with a bigger base. Sure, a pyramid took longer to build, but my long-term satisfaction skyrocketed when the structure was three times taller than my skinny block tower and was still standing the next day.

A major theme in weight loss and fitness is the idea of using short cuts and getting to the end result as quickly as possible - building your block tower straight up. We are constantly bombarded with gimmicks like, *Solar Abs!; 5 Minutes to a Rockin' Bod!; B12 injections for weight loss!* and *Super Sculpting Supplements!* These may help you to build a skinny block tower toward your goals, but gains are typically short-lived and unsustainable. Lasting results come with proper diet, performing quality workouts and having our FAMS in order. At Results Fitness, our clients use the Tune Up class to build and fortify our client's bodies to reach new heights of achievement.

The beauty of the Tune Up is that you build your base WHILE you are working toward your goals. You don't need to stop your current training program. The Tune Up can be done on its own, but can also be done before or after a workout. Not only can you perform it whenever you want, but what you will gain from tuning up your body will augment the effects of your training programs.

Let's look at an example. You are a client looking for fat loss. Muscle is the biggest contributor to your resting metabolic rate (RMR). The higher your RMR, the higher your metabolism. The higher your metabolism, the more fat you burn. When you cannot use your muscles to their full potential, you are limiting how high your RMR can be. **You are limiting your fat burn.** Your tower can only be built so high. The Tune Up frees you to use your muscles to their full potential, increasing your RMR and increasing your fat burn. You will get more out of your workout and achieve your goal in less time.

I don't want you to take my word for it. This is real-life Results Fitness client Pam J. Pam had worked hard and lost a lot of weight.

As far as reaching her fat loss goals, it seemed Pam had "made it," but like many people she still had her fair share of aches and pains and hit plateaus when she tried to progress in her work outs. Pam built a tall skinny block tower. One false move and the tower would crumble, causing pain and limiting her exercise potential. It was time to build a base around what she had achieved so that she could move beyond her plateau.

As a physical therapist, I have had the pleasure of working with her to address her pain. We have successfully used the Tune Up during her treatment and after discharge to keep her feeling good and increase her exercise ability. When we started, Pam was unable to squat without pitching over to her right side or hyperextending her low back. Now Pam has progressed to full squatting, dead-lifting and swinging kettle-bells. "The Tune Up teaches me how to move and exercise properly. I have become aware of how my body moves, what my body should feel like when I exercise correctly. I can now catch and correct myself when I lose form. This keeps my pain level low and I know I'm helping and not hurting myself," says Pam.

True success in any weight loss or fitness program is maintaining the effects of the program. Success = building a tower that is durable and will stand the test of time. Most people have yo-yo'd in their fitness levels. Avoiding burnout and keeping motivated to stick with a program is crucial in reaching fitness goals and sustaining weight loss. "Where I was over 200 lbs. ago to where I am now is a mental game. Do I like going to the gym? No, but the gym is like another family to me and the Tune Up helps me to stay motivated internally." Having a strong mind-body connection helps Pam to re-charge her batteries, reinforces that she is doing the right things for her body and keeps her motivated to keep the weight off.

"The Tune Up allows me to get in touch with my body, my posture and how my body moves. I know what my body should feel like when I exercise correctly and I am better able to communicate with my trainer about what I am feeling and what I am looking for in my customized program. Knowing that I am performing my exercises correctly gives me a mental edge. I can feel that what I am doing is healthy."

On average people are on their best behavior for the three hours a week they are in the gym. Clients get cues from their trainers and pay extra attention to what they are feeling, but what about when they are at home or work? What happens during the 165 hours away from a watchful eye? Becoming aware of your body and the way it should move is a huge benefit to the Tune Up class, helping you to take what you learn and apply it to everyday life. For example, Pam has become more aware of when her body is not aligned properly. She can now catch herself compensating during everyday activities. "I can feel when I start slouching or leaning to one side while driving. I tell myself to sit up and bring my shoulders back and down." At home, Pam no longer sits on her couch, noting, "I became aware that the couch was causing me to slouch leading to my back pain." Now she is able to enjoy making her crafts without pain.

UNLEASH THE POWER OF YOUR BODY:

Think about your smart phone. When you don't know that you have all the bells and whistles that go along with the phone, you will use it just to call people. Once you are educated on how the phone works, you can realize its full potential. The possibilities seem endless. You can text, download apps, translate a foreign language, answer emails, play games, find the nearest 5-star restaurant and oh yeah, you can still call someone. Tuning Up your body helps you to learn what your body can do, and teaches you how to use it. In Pam's experience she has learned that, "if you are aware of how your body moves and you gain an understanding of your muscles and how they move, it will help you physically for the rest of your life. Being aware of what you can do to help yourself will ultimately change your physical abilities. "The Tune Up has made me so in tune with my body.

Before I would think, 'Do I really have muscles there?' Now I can access them and use them to my advantage. This has made my work outs more effective and my sex life more satisfying."

So when and how do you do this program? Again, you can perform the Tune Up on its own, before or after a workout. Not only can you Tune Up whenever you want, but you can do it as much as you want. At least one Tune Up a week is recommended, but you can still get benefits from going through the program periodically.

Prior to your training program, a Tune Up will prepare your body to move the best it can. This allows you to get more out of your training session. Post workout, the Tune Up promotes recovery from training stress. "After a workout, the Tune Up helps my body relax and I feel stretched out," says Pam. An intense workout can leave you feeling exhausted, but when followed by a Tune Up, you leave the gym feeling energized and put back together.

This program can also be done independent of your workout. "I use it as a way to train internally and regroup, keeping me on my mental game, connecting the mind and body," says Pam. It offers a different kind of challenge than your normal workouts. You won't 'gas out' your body with this program, but you may feel what I like to call a "neurologic" tired. You are re-wiring how you use your body which may be a bit of a task, but when complete, the signals gets from your brain to your muscles much smoother.

So lets get to it! This is an example of a Tune Up class:

Each class begins with self-massage, stretching and activation techniques listed as "Mobility, Activation & Movement Prep." You will need a foam roll and lacrosse (LAX) ball for this section. After this section is completed, move on to the exercise circuits. Each circuit is 8 minutes long and has 3 exercises. You will repeat these exercises in order until the 8 minutes is up, then move on to the next circuit. Rest periods between circuits are 0-1 minute based on individual necessity. Regressions are built in and written next to each exercise. Go at your own pace. Remember it is about quality, not quantity.

For video instruction on this Tune Up program, please visit our YouTube channel at: http://www.youtube.com/user/Resultsftns

Vince Lombardi, a great American football coach is credited with

	Results Fitness Group Coaching						
Order	Mobility, Activation & Movement Prep	Sets	Reps		Tune-up 10		
	LAX: Upper body, QL, Piriformis	1	10ea				
	Foam roll: Calves, Hams, Thoracic extension, Angels	1	10ea				
	supine 2 position Hamstring stretch, Calf on wall,	1	20 sec				
	Seated glute stretch with rotaiton and deep breath	1	20 sec				
Order	8 min circuits. 8 reps or breaths ea SLOW	Regressions:					
1a	SA Band Traction Lat stretch	seated QL stretch					
1b	Band Ws with elbow drive	Prone I or T					
1c	Supine T-rotation	sidelying diagonal reach					
2a	kneeling hip flexor FFE	knee pain = Standing at wall					
2b	figure 4 SL hip bridge	passoce lock SL hip bridge or double leg hip bridge					
2c	1/2 kneeling hi-lo chops	knee pain = split stance; Cue: light front foot					
3a	TRX pec stretch	foam roll supine lying					
3b	Rolling - upper body 4 each (8 total)	lower body driven					
3c	Face the wall squat	TRX or band assisted squat				Notes: Check for pain; Regress any station if necessary to accommodate.	
	Finisher: Vary int. time according to class size	Sets	Reps	Work	Recovery	Adjust number of rounds if needed for new clients.	
Regeneraton							
SMR, stretch, post workout recovery							

saying, "Practice doesn't make perfect. Perfect practice makes perfect." Each Tune Up class is designed with this in mind. The goal is to get your body to move in the best, most efficient way possible. Remember it is about quality, not quantity. The better you move the more you can accomplish.

Now the only question is: What do YOU want to achieve?

About Amy

Amy Wunsch, MSPT is part of the founder of Results Physical Therapy, a division of Results Fitness and the Tune Up program. Amy received two Masters Degrees in Clinical Science and Physical Therapy from Ithaca College where she was a captain of the New York State Champion Women's Indoor and Outdoor Track and Field teams and a member of the NCAA Finalist Women's Soccer Team. She is licensed in the state of California and is a proud member of the American Physical Therapy Association with special interests in orthopedic rehabilitation and sport rehabilitation. Amy has experience working with recreational, professional and Olympic athletes, stunt-people, celebrities, Cirque du Soleil performers as well as patients with orthopedic, lymphedema, cardiac, post-surgical and neurologic conditions ranging from 7-weeks-old to 94 years of age.

Dedicated to excellence and continuing education, Amy has received her certification in Functional Movement Systems I and II and Selective Functional Movement Assessment. She is certified by the Titleist Performance Institute and lectures to an international audience. Amy is a Best-Selling author who has also been featured in *Experience Life Magazine* and *Women's Health Magazine.*

Results Physical Therapy exists to make a difference in the local and global communities through supplying the highest quality of care and educational opportunities. Amy Wunsch, MSPT and the Results Team are focused reaching patient goals, exceeding expectations and realizing their patient's full potential.

Website: www.results-fitness.com

Work Phone: 661-799-7900

CHAPTER 3

IT ALL STARTS HERE – The Achievement Mindset

BY BRETT A. RIESENHUBER, BS, CPPT

INTRODUCTION

"Hey, are you going to eat your fat?"
-Spalding in "Caddy Shack"

You ever been fat? Maybe right now?

Ever felt fat? Maybe right now?

Get this...Our bodies actually LIKE to be fat! Can you believe that! It's true, the more fat we have, the better suited we are for the next famine that is right around the corner (if you've been a "yo-yo" dieter, then you know what I'm talking about here). In pre-historic times, famine was always a possibility, and the human body was designed a long time ago!

Truth is that the body doesn't get it, the only famine we have nowadays is the one we self-inflict with fad diets every month or two. Having too much fat and being uncomfortable and unhappy SUCKS! Trust me here, I've been battling the bulge for the past 29 years (OK...we know by the grey in my beard, and hair, that the 29 thing is a myth...so let's just say that I'm around whatever age you are).

Yep, I've spent a lifetime battling body fat and feeling crappy about how I look. Even when I'm in great shape, I still suck in my gut! And I've spent more than 2 decades (if you still buy the 29 years old thing, then I started my professional fitness for fat loss coaching career at 15!) coaching my clients on how to be successful in losing weight, and keeping it off.

Hell, I've got a great testing ground...myself! (I've also coached <u>thousands</u> of people how to do it right.)

My gym, Prime Physique Fitness (soon to become Achievement Fitness) in San Jose, California for 20 years, has one goal:

"Changing lives, one body at a time by providing more than just a workout."

And that begins from within our team of coaches, and extends out to every member of the gym, my Adventure Boot Camp for Women, and my loyal blog and email subscribers (I'll share the secrets for getting into the "Inner Circle" later).

You see, it all began when I changed my own life. I wasn't an athlete...I was a regular guy who was way out of shape, packing on way too many pounds... I was a fat kid with a weight problem, and somehow I got into lifting weights. I loved lifting, I just sort of had an instinct for it and this instinct combined with my love of coaching and helping others succeed, launched my career that has span more than 2 decades (so far).

And guess what? I still screw up and get off the path occasionally!

Then I coach myself right back. The system I've developed works, even for me, and I'm going to share some of the mindset parts of my weight loss system with you! Then you will have the basis for transforming your body and changing your life!

THE MIND SHIFT

"I will not let anyone walk through my mind with their dirty feet."
- Mahatma Gandhi

Every body transformation begins with one thing, the proper mindset. The secret is simple; know what the mindset changes are that need to be made, implement these changes in your daily life, and continually train yourself to use your new-found tools.

Words Are Everything

There is one word in the English vocabulary that can be declared to be "the worst word we have in the entire English language," and that is the word "should." The word "should" is just an all-around crappy word to use, and completely disempowers you EVERY time it's used.

The word "should" is total copout. You know you "should" do something. But now, since you said, "I should," you have actually created an excuse not to it! When you "should" do something, your mind nonchalantly takes "non-action" as being acceptable.

The word "should" is nothing more than an excuse word. So drop it from your vocabulary. Never say it again. Now obviously we need a replacement for the word "should" so… change your way of thinking.

What should we use to replace "that word?" (Don't say it!) The best two words that come to mind are "will" and "must." There's no gray area with these two words. If you "must" do something, then there is no choice involved. **You must do it.** When you "will" do something, once again no gray area. **You will do it.**

There Is Always A Solution

Now that we've taken out the number one excuse word, and replaced it with two powerful action-taking words, let's go to work on how to change. Be ready for everything. Guess what? Something **will** get in your way. The cool thing is, there's <u>always</u>

a solution to every problem.

This simple three-step process gets the ball rolling:

1. Identify the problem
2. Identify a solution and
3. Implement.

More simply put... When obstacles get in your way, turn, and keep moving forward. Let's take a look at a scenario...

You're going out to run an errand today. Not a big deal, just an errand that should take an hour or so. But one errand turns into two, and then you run into a friend, and the next thing you know four hours have past and you're hungry. When you get hungry, your willpower drops, along with your blood sugar. Solution becomes easy...Fast food!

Oops...Diet blown with a 1200-calorie fast food meal. Well we know fast food is never the solution that will help you to change your body for the better, so your program just got derailed.

Now let's rethink this situation, and plan for success! Remember, there's always a solution, you just have to be ready for it and think ahead. What if you plan for the possibility of your original plan not going right? You throw a small cooler into your car with some simple food packed in it. Maybe an apple, a small bag of nuts, a couple pieces of string cheese, and a bottle of water. Now if something changes in your plan, you're still prepared to stay on your program! And if everything goes right and you are only out for an hour, you can put the food back in the refrigerator when you get home.

Oftentimes the best solutions can be found with a little bit of help, another set of eyes, which is where Coach comes in... More on that later.

Powerful Thinking Rocks

We've all heard about having a positive mindset. This is no fluff about be happy and everything will be great...BUT what you <u>say</u> **and** what you <u>think</u> does drive your mindset. What do I mean by this?

Your mindset has a direct impact on the direction in which your mind leads you, at a subconscious level. If you tell yourself that you <u>can't</u> do something, you are absolutely correct, you can't and won't. You can't because you've just programmed your mind to believe you can't! If you tell yourself that some part of your body is weak, then you are right. You just confirmed it in your mind, and you will be weak.

But what if you simply tweaked your mind and words a little bit with these positive thoughts:

- "I'm <u>going</u> to be able to do that."

- "My core is <u>getting stronger</u>."

- "My left arm is <u>becoming</u> as strong as my right."

- "My butt is getting smaller with every workout, and with every successful change I make to my diet each week." (Yea baby, this one ROCKS!)

You are kind of saying the same thing, but now you've restructured the words to **become** <u>positive and self-serving</u>... as opposed to negative and self-defeating. Changing the way we think takes time and effort. Working with a coach who understands can certainly help...I'm always working with clients on just this piece. I even work with my wife on this regularly... AND, in turn, she kicks my butt sometimes too!

But that's what it is all about, we are all "real people" with real life challenges...and the best way to accomplish it is on a team. That's what we build at Achievement Fitness, a team of support, all working together to achieve our goals.

ACTION MADE EASY

"Go that way, really fast. If something gets in your way, turn."
-Better Off Dead (Movie)

One Step At A Time

It's easy for me, or any professional fitness coach, to give you a complete plan for weight loss and body transformation success. We live this stuff and can blab on and on. The problem is that we can only handle making a few changes at a time, and then we hit "overload." When overload hits, it's like hitting a wall on your bike...you are pretty much done riding!

The secret is to take everything **one step at a time**. Each step of your process is taken, packed into your brain, and formed into habit. Only then you are ready to add the next step. Take one step every week.

Step 1: Get a great workout program and start it. That probably involves hiring a coach, but that is up to you. Take a week and get into a habit of going to the gym and exercising in your new program.

Step 2: Start tracking your food. Start this one the second week. Nothing big, just tracking. Your coach probably gave you a nutrition guide; so read it several times too.

Step 3: Make ONE change to your diet. Just one change. So show your journal to your coach, get feedback, and pick one thing to work on that week.

Step 4-52: Add one more step each week, while maintaining the actions you took the previous weeks...next thing you know, you have made 52 changes (a year), and you have a new life, a new lifestyle, and a new body!

You Still Will Screw Up

So you've been consistent with your weekly changes, and you are working out regularly...then BAM!

Your friends all went out, and they took you along for the ride. You told them that you want to stay on your program, but as soon as they heard that... They declared (in their minds) "Game on!"

What game? The "get-you-off-your-program-game." The "get-you-down-to-my-level-game!" And you completely went off your program! You had the sugary cocktails, the bread, and the fried appetizers.... Oh, and the wine too.

You pigged out and totally blew your diet plan! Hey...You WILL Screw Up. It is OK. Actually an occasional splurge is necessary for your diet success. Tell yourself that it's OK, and get back on your program immediately. It does not matter what day it is, or what time of day, get back on your program. You cheated! It's not high school, an occasional cheat is fine.

Welcome to the real world, we like pizza!

ACHIEVEMENT PROGRAM 101

"My most brilliant achievement was my ability to be able to persuade my wife to marry me."
-Winston Churchill

Know That You MUST Workout

You MUST workout, with weights. Sorry to be the first in this book to burst the cardio bubble, but cardio falls far below weight training and diet when it comes to weight/fat loss. Resistance training builds lean muscle tone, increases your metabolism, makes you stronger, fitter, and happier. Weight training is the cornerstone to your weight loss program.

AND... weight training lets you eat more! How cool is that!?!?

Know That You MUST Diet

You can't out train a crappy diet …My favorite quote.

You MUST watch your diet, and you must be compliant 90% of the time. And yes, I said DIET; your diet is the way you eat. You need to be on a specific diet plan that gets results for your body. Diet is not a bad word.

Know That You MUST Get Your Sleep

Sleep? How does sleep fit into the equation? When we sleep, our bodies are rebuilding, repairing, regenerating, and recovering from exercise. Without adequate sleep, the body cannot adequately recover and change.

Make sure to get at least 6 hours of sleep every night, 8 is usually better.

EVERYONE NEEDS A COACH

"Coaching is a profession of love.
You can't coach people unless you love them."
-Eddie Robinson

Know That You MUST HAVE A Coach

The best players in every sport have a coach. The best coaches have a coach. The best of the best of the best...have a coach. Most of the best have multiple coaches.

Know that you MUST have a coach too. And you too may have more than one coach, it's ok.

Quality Is Key

Coaches help you see things that you wouldn't look at, and in a way that you might have never seen. A high quality, experienced coach helps you stay focused, holds you accountable, and gets you to break past barriers while assisting you from sabotaging your results.

Systems Produce Results

Systems work, every time. Great coaches have systems that get results. You follow the system, you get results. When something isn't working, you probably deviated from the system, or it is time to move to the next phase of the program...and that's in the system!

Be sure your coach has a "system," or run like hell! I can't tell you the number of times I've experienced personal trainers, boot camp programs, or other fitness programs that simply go with a random approach, such as a "workout of the day" where every day the program is different, and I mean EVERY DAY! There is no system there...just a "fly by the seat of your pants" approach to your exercise program.

Find a great coach...he/she/the team will lead you to the Promised Land, and you will achieve your goals, and transform your body and mind. You will be happy, balanced, and have time for yourself to work on the most important person in the world: YOU.

Think about that for one second, the most important person in the world is **YOU**. Go ahead and argue that for a second...My kids are the most important! My _____ (fill in the blank) is the most important person.

The Truth: When **you** make time for yourself to get better, when **you** make yourself the most important, **you** allow yourself to grow, get healthier, get stronger, get leaner, be happier, be more confident, have higher self esteem, and live a better life. **You** will be able to care for the person/people in your life who **are** the most important at an even higher level. **You** will contribute to their lives at the highest level possible, because **you** WILL be happier. They want what's best for **you** too...so do I.

Live your great life with one achievement after another and you will be able to give back more than you ever dreamed!

About Brett

Widely regarded as one of America's most innovative fitness professionals, Brett Riesenhuber has been coaching and training for twenty-two years. The breakthrough results Brett helps people achieve are largely driven by giving his clients a new way to think. From his own lifelong experience battling weight challenges, Brett created an effective way to channel the powerful role that mindset and attitude play in getting results.

Brett was not an athlete growing up. "I was a regular guy who was way out of shape, packing on way too many pounds. I was a fat kid with a weight problem, and somehow I got into lifting weights. I loved lifting, I just sort of had an instinct for it, and this instinct combined with my love of coaching and helping others succeed, launched my career."

The programs Brett creates helps people lose weight, keep it off, and recapture lost energy. Each one is designed to give people a simple way to not only lose weight and transform their body, but also to transform their lives. Brett says, "Do you ever wonder why so many folks go to the gym who don't really want to be there? Well, the people who come to our gym aren't like this at all. They have developed an outlook that completely changes the nature of their commitment to fitness. If you're going to get with the program, the best place to start is by getting your mindset squared away."

Brett earned his Bachelor's degree in Movement Science from San Jose State University in 1994 and is a certified Functional Movement Screen (FMS) and Corrective Exercise professional. He is also a certified Russian Kettlebell instructor and has been certified as a TRX Suspension trainer.

He is the founder and owner of Prime Physique Fitness, soon to become Achievement Fitness, and Adventure Boot Camp for Women in San Jose, California. Brett's mission: "Changing lives, one body at a time by providing more than just a workout." Brett was named 'Personal Trainer of the Year' by the San Jose Mercury News in 2010. He captured the 'Number One Personal Trainer' award by the *Campbell Times*, *Cambrian Times*, and *Willow Glen Times* from 2008-2011, and in 2009 and 2010, Prime Physique Fitness and San Jose Adventure Boot Camp were voted 'The Best of Silicon Valley' by the *Metro*.

The innovative approach Brett has refined over the years is designed for people who live busy lives, and are looking for a more fulfilling experience, greater balance, and improved health.

"For years, I've wanted to get my approach down on paper. I've wanted to give people I may never have the opportunity to meet a simple, proven, and effective way to take control of their weight challenges. Now, with the publication of *Get With The Program*, folks can understand that the thoughts they think, the beliefs they hold, and the attitude they embrace are the true foundations for success."

Brett and his wife Denise live in San Jose, California.

For more information, go to:
www.achievementfitness.com/getwiththeprogram

CHAPTER 4

EXECUTIVE FITNESS: A PROFESSIONAL'S GUIDE TO QUICK EFFECTIVE WORKOUTS

BY BRIAN BOTT

It's 5:30 am, the alarm goes off and you roll out of bed. You shower, get dressed, and if you're lucky, grab a cup of coffee and you're out the door to start your commute. Once you get to the office you have just enough time to grab a bagel with some cream cheese before your 8:00 am meeting. You're stuck in a chair for the first 6 hours of the day, and again if you're lucky, you hit up the fast food joint across the street with co-workers and get right back to work. You return to the office, pick up that mid-afternoon coffee with cream and sugar to get through the rest of the day and you're back to the chair. It's 6:00 pm and you finally arrive home. Sure it'd be great to get a quick workout in to blow off some steam from a long workday, but the kids have a soccer game you are already late to, so you blow it off until tomorrow. It's now 8:00 pm and you are exhausted. You grab a quick dinner with the family and by now it's time for bed. You tell yourself, "I'll start tomorrow" and hit the sack. You'll get up and go the gym early before work, or you'll grab a quick workout at the office gym during lunch, maybe even stop at the gym before coming home. You finally do make it to the gym and do your best to get a quick 30-minute cardio workout in, because let's be honest, when you are short on time, it's the easiest thing to do. You manage to keep this up for a few weeks only to realize your weight hasn't changed, your clothes don't fit any better, and more importantly you start to feel like YOUR valuable time is being wasted.

While training clients over the past 10 years, the above story is by far the most common I hear when new members consult our services. Early in my career, I would rarely listen and try to understand the situation my clients were in. I would design them a lifting routine that required them to come to the gym 4-5 times per week, following bodybuilding-type lifting routines that could take upwards of 1.5 to 2 hours. When the client didn't show up and wasn't getting results I would take the easy way out, blame their lack of adherence to the program and insist that I was giving them the best advice possible. Fast forward a few years, and I had built up a successful training business, one that often required me to start my day with 6:00 am clients and often not finishing up to around 8 or 9 pm. Even if I had a break during the middle of the day, it was spent writing client programs. Before I knew it, I was 10-15 lbs. heavier, not nearly as strong or in shape as I once was, and often found myself pushing back workouts to make sure I completed all of my personal and business obligations. I couldn't believe it... the roles had been reversed, and I was now in the same situation that 80 percent of my clients were in. I was forced to adapt and decided I needed to eliminate all the fluff from my training sessions and only program in what was absolutely necessary to produce the results I was looking for. It was from this self-realization that the "Executive Fitness" program was born. I took the next few days and looked back over the characteristics of the majority of my clients and produced the following list. If you are anything like me, you'll find several of these describe you and your situation quite well.

CHARACTERISTICS OF THE FITNESS EXECUTIVE.

1. Extremely successful in your professional/personal life but struggle with the frustration of "failing" at your health and fitness goals.

2. You are the man/woman in charge, so the thought of being told what to do by someone else is a bit of a challenge.

3. Extremely motivated and organized in your professional work, but approach your workouts with a lack of planning or real focus.

4. You choose to do cardio over lifting because it's the easiest thing to just get in and do.

5. You think you get enough lower body work from your running.

6. You still like a good challenge. Jumping in a weekend 5k, paddle-boarding, mud-runs, trail-runs and mountain biking are all things you may like to do in your free time to satisfy your competitive nature.

7. You're jacked up… that's a technical term. The last time you stretched or did mobility work was the jumping jacks your high school football coach made you do. Your active lifestyle has left you with some sort of nagging injury that forces you to be just a little bit more careful than you used to with your training.

8. Finally, your free time, family, and business are extremely important to you and anything that is going to take time away from any of those MUST be valuable and produce results or it will be put to the wayside.

So with the above considerations, my team and myself at Shore Results have developed a program that can solve most of your problems. Its easy to follow, gives you the freedom to pick which exercises you will be using, and gets you in and out of the gym in about 30 minutes.

Your workouts will be broken down in to four parts:

(i). Mobility/Warmup (5 minutes)
This section focuses on loosening up some of the joints and muscles that stiffen up from the hours spent seated during your commute or desk chair. Note: DO NOT skip this step. For some of you this will be just as much of a workout as the other sections.

(ii). Strength (10minutes)
The goal here focuses on getting stronger at some of the core movements. The goal here is to use the most weight possible that you can complete the movement with good form.

(iii). Metabolic Resistance Training (15minutes)
Here we will pick three exercises, two upper and one lower body movement. Due to postural considerations you will ALWAYS perform some sort of upper body pulling movement. The goal here is to get as much work done as we can in 10-15 minutes – either by increasing the weight, reps, or sets we shoot to improve each time.

(iv). Finishers (<5 minutes)
Here is where you get to put your need to set personal records to the test. The 5 finishers I will list for you will each provide their own unique challenge that allows you to track progress each time you do one.

SCHEDULING WORKOUTS

What I've found to work better for busy clients is to schedule more frequent short workouts rather than just a few long sessions. It allows us to keep the intensity high which improves the quality of the workout. It leads to greater adherence, as you will be less likely to skip the workout knowing it will only take you 30-45 minutes as opposed to 60-90.

So to keep it simple, I'd like you to try to schedule at least 3 of these workouts per week. Due to the short intense nature of the workouts, you COULD perform up to 5 of these per week if you found yourself with extra time.

DESIGNING THE WORKOUT

Part 1- Mobility /Warmup

This will be the most tempting part of the workout to skip however it could be argued to be the most important. Whether it is your commute or the hours you spend at your desk, you are spending a majority of your day in a seated position that is stiffening up your hips and upper back and putting you at a greater risk for back and shoulder pain when beginning to exercise.

While everyone we see in our gym is screened and there are prescribed specific drills for them based on their own unique limitations, I've selected four of the most basic drills we use with almost all of our clients with desk jobs.

1. **Hip Flexor-Quad Stretch w/ Reach** – For this stretch get on one knee placing the foot of the knee that is down up on a bench or box. Try to make yourself as tall as possible and squeeze the glute of the down leg attempting to push your hip forward. To increase the stretch reach the arm on the same side of the leg that is down toward the ceiling. Perform 30s hold on each side.

2. **6 Point TSpine Rotation** – Assume the 6 point position (hands and knees) keeping your hands under your shoulders and knees under your hips. Start by taking one hand off the ground trying to reach toward the ceiling by turning your chest to be perpendicular to the floor. Use the arm that is still on the ground to help push yourself to get a greater range of motion. Perform 10 reps on each side.

3. Single Leg Bridge – Sitting on your butt all day lends itself to tight hip flexors which we addressed with the first stretch and poorly functioning glutes. This next drill helps get you reacquainted with how to use these muscles correctly. Lying on your back with your knees bent and feet flat on the floor simply bring one knee as close to your chest as possible. From this position simply push through the heel of the down foot and squeeze your butt up to the ceiling and hold for a count of 2. Perform 10 reps of 2-second holds on each side.

4. Wall Slides – The other side effect of slouching all day at your desk is poor slouching posture and weak overstretched stabilizing muscles in your upper back. This next exercise will look very easy but if performed correctly can be very challenging and lead to great improvements in posture. Stand flat back against a wall. You can adjust your feet distance from the wall as needed but make sure your entire back is flat. With your palms facing forward, place your arms flat against the wall. Keeping EVERYTHING flat against the wall reach your arms up the wall while gently pushing back against it. From the top, keep pressure against the wall and slide your arms back down. You should feel all the muscles in your upper back and shoulders starting to light up. Just make sure you keep your lower back from arching up off of the wall. Perform one set of 12 reps.

Part 2 – Strength

Ok for the first part of this section you are only going to pick ONE movement from this list. If you pick an upper body movement for your first workout you must pick a lower body for your next workout. The letters after each exercise will make more sense later on.

Upper Body Exercises	Lower Body Exercises
Bench Press (A)	Back Squat (A)
Incline Bench Press (A)	Front Squat (A)
DB Bench Press (A)	Goblet Squat (A)
Standing Military Press (B)	Deadlift (B)
Close Grip Bench Press (B)	Partial Range Deadlift (B)

I'd like you to keep performing warmup sets until you reach a difficult set of 10 repetitions. This should be a weight that you feel like you could have only done for another rep but DO NOT go to failure. I then want you to add a little weight and perform 8 reps. Then do a final set where you add just a little bit more weight for 6 reps. So 3 sets... Set 1: 10 Reps; Set 2: 8 reps; Set 3: 6 reps. Keep a log book for yourself and each time you return to an exercise try to beat your previous exercise. As a general rule, do not repeat the same exercise more than 1x per week.

Part 3 - Metabolic Resistance Training

Here you will pick two exercises, one from the Upper Body list and one from the Lower Body List. If for your strength exercise you picked an exercise labeled (A) you must pick an upper body exercise in this section labeled (A). Each Group has exercises that could suit either pairing.

Upper Body Push	Lower Body Exercises
DB Military Press (A)	Step Ups (A)
Single Arm DB Push Press (A)	KB Swings (A)
Double Medicine Ball Pushups (A/B) (one hand on each)	Walking Lunges (A/B)
DB Bench Press (B)	Rear Foot Elevated Split Squats (B)
Feet Elevated Pushups (A/B)	Goblet Squats (B)

Upper Body Pulling (Pick one)	
3 Point DB Row	Chinups/ Pullups
Standing Cable Rows	Wide Grip Lat Pulldown
Bent Over Rows	Underhand Lat Pulldown
Inverted Rows	Neutral Grip Lat Pulldown

After selecting your exercises, set a timer for 10 to 15 minutes depending on what you have available. You will perform the exercises in the order of Upper Pull – Lower – Upper Push. Choose a weight that is difficult but not maximum for 10 reps… this will take some experimentation at first. After that it's press start and go. You will perform as many rounds of the three exercises you chose in the 10- to 15-minute time period. Again, keep a log book for yourself and focus each time on trying to make small improvements on weight used and rounds performed.

Part 4 - Finishers

Here's where we use simple movements and try to beat a previous record/ time each time. Below are the five most commonly used by our fitness executives in Shore Results:

1. **Jump Squat/ Pushup Countdowns** – You will perform this as fast as possible. You will perform 10 jump squats followed by 10 pushups; 9 jump squats followed by 9 pushups… Continue until you reach the bottom and record your time.

2. **KB Swings 5 minute Rep Challenge** – Set a timer for 5 minutes. With an appropriate load perform as many reps as possible. If you get more than 120reps choose a heavier weight.

3. **1 Mile "Sprint"** – Again we favor movements we can time and improve. This one is simple and straight forward… just keep improving.

4. 1000m Row – This is a great challenge if your gym has a rowing machine. Set the distance for 1000m and get after it.

5. Burpee Challenge – Set a timer on repeat for 30 seconds... for 5 minutes you will do as many burpees in 30 seconds as you can, followed by a 30 second rest period. Tally up your reps over the 5 rounds and try to improve each time.

PUTTING IT ALL TOGETHER...
REAL LIFE EXAMPLE...

The following is a sample workout combining all of the above elements. This exact workout was used by one of my client's, Dave. Dave is General Manager of Bedminster Golf Club, which just finished second for best course in the country. So as you can imagine, Dave is a busy guy. Here's a typical AM workout for Dave if he has to be out in a rush:

1. Warmup – Exactly as above

2. Strength – Trap Bar Deadlift- 185x10; 195x8; 210x6

3. Metabolic Resistance Training – (15 minutes)
    a. Chin-ups - 4 sets of 6
    b. Rear Foot Elevated Split squat - 4 sets of 10 each leg
    c. Double Med Ball Pushups - 4 sets of 10 Reps (with weight-vest)

4. Finisher – 1000m Row - Just under 4 minutes

This workout took only 45 minutes and covered nearly all major muscle groups and facets of training.

There are only so many hours of the day, and time is our only non-renewable resource. Planning time for fitness is not easy but I hope that I've simplified that for you with the details in this chapter. Take the focus and vision that has made you so successful in your professional career and simply apply the templates you have been given. For more information you can visit my website at: www.brianbott.com

Best of luck in your fitness journey and keep moving forward!

About Brian

Brian Bott is a 2003 graduate of Rutgers University and earned a Bachelor's Degree in Exercise Physiology with High Honors.

Brian has helped a tremendous number of clients over the last ten years realize their full potential in achieving their health and fitness goals. Constantly refining and improving his techniques in all aspects of training, coaching, nutrition and personal assessment has brought Brian to the program he now utilizes at Shore Results, located in Atlantic Highlands, NJ. This program was responsible for producing nearly 500 lbs. of fat loss in Shore Result's latest transformation challenge.

Brian holds two Elite Powerlifting totals in the AAPF with personal best lifts of a 725 lb. squat, 455 lb. bench, and 585 lb. deadlift. He now competes in bodybuilding and recently finished 2nd in the lightweight division of his first competition in the INBF.

Brian can be reached for coaching at his gym, Shore Results, located in Atlantic Highlands, NJ or via his website at: www.brianbott.com or www.shore-results.com

CHAPTER 5

TRAINING WOMEN WHO ARE UNDER EXTREME STRESS

BY CHRIS OLMSTEAD

What first attracted me to the gym wasn't the appeal of lifting heavy weights, the great body composition changes or even the marked strength increases, even though those were always the things I measured my progress by. For me it was always the environment. The camaraderie enjoyed at the gym and the support from my "gym friends" who were often my "outside the gym friends" too. In fact, I liked it enough to make a career out of it, to let others get out of it my favorite part. That's what I always thought the gym was really for; developing a sense of community within a small group of people who simply want to improve their lives.

During my years in the fitness industry, I have had the opportunity to work with many women going through very difficult times in their lives. Sometimes they have come to me as a client because of these transitions, and sometimes they have simply been with me as a client during these transitions. Some of these very difficult trials have been divorce, death of a loved one, or loss of a job. And that's what I wanted to write about; helping women get through these tough transitional phases of life and making sure they keep going, and, more importantly, are still able to enjoy the gym.

During an interview for this chapter, my client Olivia mentioned to me the biggest problem was all the uncertainty involved with going through her divorce. Not knowing where she was going to be living during and after the divorce, how to deal with loss of income and how she was going to pay for all her living expenses, and most importantly, what was going to happen with her kids. While she was going through this life change, she told me the gym was a big safe haven for her. It was a place to escape all the negativity surrounding her and be surrounded by people who only cared about her and helping her feel better. It was a constant in her life rather than a variable. She reported looking forward to the accountability, to the stress relief and the feeling of control and stability it provided her.

"What really kept me going was the sense of community in there. For years I had all our 'couples friends,' and then during the divorce they started to take sides and go away. But I had my gym friends and they knew what I was going through and that was very encouraging for me! I think my favorite part, and it always has been, was that I got to be prioritized by somebody else, instead of having to think about myself last."

Another client, Patty, was going through her own very stressful time with her new job. "I was a relatively new CPA for this accounting firm, and not doing the type of accounting I had been trained to do and really missed. Come tax season, I was working 60 plus hours every week for 10 weeks straight, doing something I hated and my life was becoming very miserable, very quickly. I didn't get to spend as much time with my daughters, I felt like my house was turning into a disaster zone and I felt like I had no time to plan anything out! I had to convince myself to get into the gym and every time I did, I always walked out feeling better. The workouts were modified for me and based on what I was willing and not willing to do on that day. Sometimes we did something entirely off the script! Not once did I regret coming, although I do regret the times I didn't."

Audrey told me she joined during the end of her three-year divorce process and in the middle of her house being foreclosed on due to all the financial entanglements. "The gym was a place I could go to just to breathe. I was surrounded by all sorts of uncertainty outside of the gym, kids, living arrangements and all the emotional relationship stuff which would just make me feel suffocated. The gym was a great outlet for all my stress. When I felt like I wasn't in control of so many parts of my life at the time, I got to feel like I was in control here. I got to control my body, I got to control the weight. And I got to throw stuff too! It made me feel strong and powerful and reminded me of my independence."

One of the common threads all of my clients have had when going through all these life- changing scenarios is uncertainty and, to some extent, a feeling of anger. They're uncertain what their future holds and uncertain how they're going to change it and uncertain if they can change it. Angry because they blame themselves at some level, angry because they feel isolated all of a sudden, and angry because, damn it, they don't deserve this! And that's where a compassionate gym can be a great asset. When they come in to the facility and they wear the stresses of the day not only in their expression, but in the very way they are walking, perhaps putting a barbell on their back isn't going to help them feel better. Maybe they just need a few minutes to breathe, a few minutes to vent and a few minutes be in control. And that's exactly what all these high-stress clients report, "The gym was a place where I could control something and I got to feel like I accomplished something good for me."

*Side note to all personal trainers who train women: The secret to listening is to simply **SHUT UP.** I feel like I could end this chapter here and improve most trainers' client retention and income drastically with those two words. Often a guy's instinct is to fix the problem when a woman simply wants to relate her problem to you. **SHUT UP** and listen! Listen to what comes out of their mouth and listen to what their bodies are trying to tell* *you. That's 7 years of every day training experience I am giving to you in two words.*

A common variation of the conversation I would have with a client when they came in under these circumstances would be something along the lines of, "Hi Patty, how's it going today?"

"Miserable Chris. Horrible, awful, terrible. Everybody hates me and I'm pretty sure I hate them all back today."

"…K. Well, let's put you on the roller and let you work out some of that stress you need to get out."

"I dunno. I only came in to say I wasn't going to workout today. I just want to go home and melt into the couch."

"OK. Well, let's do something good for you before sending you home. Let's just lay down on the roller and let you do that. A cheap massage before hitting the couch, loosen up the kinks in your back a bit, maybe stretch your hips a bit too. I mean, you're already here, right?"

"Yeah, you're right. I guess I can do that. That'll be good"

After that, just figuring out what we're going to be doing is the new challenge. Are we really going to be doing just our soft tissue work? After that we can work on some breathing and help relax a bit more. Maybe even get through the RAMP? Or after the RAMP are they going to feel charged up and ready to attack the weights? If they still feel miserable but feel like they can and want to do something then what can we do that will still yield a positive result in line with their goals, temporary or not, but won't be overly stressful? The most important thing is to give yourself a chance to perform.

REDEFINING GOALS

Another aspect of training under these conditions is adjusting goals. Often times, trying to progress towards whatever original goal you may have had, fat loss, increased strength, etc., is just another stressor you may not want to deal with. Quite often, the most common goal becomes just getting into the gym. Doing this one thing you know will make you feel better. Getting into this one place where you know they will be taken care of rather than taking care of others. Simplicity is our friend.

NUTRITION

Being under extreme stress for long periods of time can often have funny effects on us. Most of us will often start craving simple carbs and sugar. It's actually a biological response. As stress levels rise a hormone called cortisol begins to rise as well. As this hormone rises our body signals for us to lower it by telling us we need foods in their most easily digestible forms, i.e., sugar and starchy carbs. Our body figures if we're feeling this way, we must need some easy form of energy and starts telling us to begin the gorging to escape that ever-dreaded sabre-toothed cat. Unfortunately when running away from the source of stress isn't the answer as it was to our caveman ancestors, we remain under that chronic stress. As this ever-prevalent stress continues and even increases at times, the signal to start the bingeing becomes stronger. During these times, it is important to stick with the simplest good nutritional habits. Drinking your water, eating that piece of fruit on your way out the door or on your way to work, down your fish oil and multi-vitamin. Pick those simplest steps and maintain them. Let simplicity be your motto regarding nutrition during these times. Keeping those positive little steps in your life will continue to give you that sense of control that is so important, and helps to contribute to your well-being.

Here's a short bullet point of the positive effects of exercise during prolonged stress *(Why Zebras Don't get Ulcers, Robert M. Sapolsky, pg. 401-402):*

- Exercise enhances mood and blunts the stress-response only for a few hours to a day after the exercise session. This means frequency is important.

- The studies have also made it clear that a more aerobic

approach to exercise during prolonged stress periods will yield greater health benefits than an anaerobic approach. This basically means leaving a few reps in the chamber and being able to talk in coherent sentences after an exercise, rather than gasping for air.

- Exercise is stress reducing so long as it is something you actually want to do. It is important that you voluntarily perform your exercise sessions rather than being forced into it.

- Exercise needs to occur on a regular basis and for a sustained period. The studies have made it clear that you need to exercise 20-30 minutes at a time, a few times per week, to really get the health benefits.

THE PROGRAM

Often times, the pre-written program will simply be too much under your current state of stress. If you are programmed to be doing a Back Squat, an exercise that can typically be loaded very heavily, then would a Front Squat be a good alternative? Maybe a Goblet Squat? Or perhaps just break it down to a Body Weight squat and let your body move in the least stressful version of that exercise. Having a knowledgeable trainer capable of building in those regressions will make a world of difference in helping you survive the day, and that is often the report I get, that these clients feel like they are in survival mode. Moderating the intensity of the session is a crucial aspect. Preventing the exertion levels from being too high will prevent a post-exercise collapse into a feeling of depression over your lack of performance. For the best ability to monitor intensity, use a heart rate monitor and keep yourself in a more aerobic work zone. It is important that we be successful with as much as we can during these times, so set yourself up for success.

Understanding that "hard and heavy" is not always going to be the best approach to your time in the gym can really be the difference between keeping the gym a positive experience, and a continued positive habit, vs. a negative experience. So, when you find yourself in one of these unfortunate scenarios, bear in mind that the gym is still a wonderful place to be and that you can still do *something*, even if it's not the designed program you walked in with. That being said, let's dig into one of those times it's OK to stray from the written program and make it an *angry workout* day!

For all my girls getting into the gym and not prepared for their designed program due to one of these extreme states, something a little more unconventional can often be exactly what the doctor ordered. They want to move, they want to throw stuff and they want to be a bit violent! Whenever I write a program, there are certain movement types I am looking to include, some sort of core exercise, a squat, a pushing and a pulling exercise, etc. So to include all these in a less conventional manner requires a little bit of creativity. Instead of a pushup or dumb bell chest press, maybe a medicine-ball chest throw to the wall. Instead of a simple plank, maybe an alligator crawl (basically a plank where you drag yourself forward on your hands). Instead of a row, how about we slam this sandbell or medicine ball into the floor. We're moving dynamically, we're being reactive to our environment, and we get to purge ourselves of some of those bad, negative emotions we've been storing all day! Most of all, it's fun! Without further ado, your program!

A Day

SMR

RAMP

A1 – Alligator walks x 20-30 yds

A2 – TRX Assisted squats or TRX assisted Squat jumps x 20

A3 – Medicine ball Chest passes x 20

A4 – Sled Sprints x 30 yds or Jump rope x 30 seconds

A5 – Overhead Medicine Ball wall Throws x 20

B Day

SMR

RAMP

A1 – Super planks x 10

A2 – KB Swings or KB Deadlifts x 20

A3 – TRX Inverted Rows x 20

A4 – Medicine ball Hip tosses x 10 each side

A5 – Medicine Ball Push Presses against wall (going for height) x 20

In each circuit take minimal rest between exercises. At the end of each, rest two minutes. Stay on your feet though! Just do a little bit of wandering around and catching your breath. Repeat each circuit 3-5 times and head home. If not using a heart monitor, regulate yourself by having a short conversation with a friend between circuits. As stated earlier, you should not be gasping for air.

The biggest take away from this program and this chapter is that, while this program can be a great deal of fun and can make for a great "finisher" to your regular program, it really is not designed to be a long-term program but simply a substitute. This program is something to help you purge the stresses from your extreme state and make you feel strong and in control of this part of your life. When life insists on being chaotic, we can still find order in the chaos from the safety of the gym.

About Chris

Chris Olmstead is the owner of Success Fitness, a gym that specializes in fat loss and is designed to focus on the individual and help each person reach their goals in the safest and fastest manner possible. Chris has travelled across the country learning from the best in the industry on how to help his clients with the most effective tools and systems possible.

Born and raised in the Salem/Keizer area, Chris has spent most of his life competing in a variety of sports, ranging from wrestling to basketball to throwing javelin. Throughout that time, he's enjoyed the benefits of the weight room and learning how to apply what he has learned there to his life, to his business and now, most importantly, to his clients.

Chris got his first taste of coaching after graduating high school and volunteering to help coach wrestling at McNary High. From there he was hooked. After attending OSU, he found his way working at a health club and was promoted to a personal trainer position where he got to really cut his teeth in the fitness end of things. After working with all manner of people from all walks of life, including the busy professional working 80+ hours per week, the stay-at-home mom and the senior citizen wanting to get stronger to stay healthy and independent, he began seeking out the best to help him improve his game. Shortly before opening Success Fitness in late 2011, Chris enrolled in the prestigious Results Fitness University and client results began improving even more.

These days, you can typically find Chris with his nose in a book, taking his dog for walks in the streets of West Salem, but mostly working with his clients at Success Fitness.

CHAPTER 6

PRACTICE WHAT YOU TEACH

BY CARMELA LIERAS LEWIS, BA

She had reached her lowest point.

That's why she was sitting across from me, clad in a baggy grey hooded sweatshirt with "University" embroidered on it, and shapeless but comfy looking sweat pants. I could tell right away that she was trying to hide what had been the accumulation of a frustrating and tested past few years. As I listened to her story, she was open, honest and pretty darn funny, which was a good sign. Granted, I could tell she wanted my help, but often times, even when we know we need it, asking for help is easier said than done, depending on the situation.

The same goes for doing the things we know we should be doing, like eating properly, getting enough sleep, and working out regularly. No matter what profession we are in, it usually feels effortless telling others what to do. Handing out advice is as easy as letting a kid roam freely through a candy store! Yet, when it comes to doing these same things ourselves, or listening to our own advice, it just doesn't happen...or at least not the way we know it should. When I first met Rae Ann, I knew that this was going to be a similar case of someone not practicing what they were preaching. In her situation, it was a matter of not practicing what she was teaching.

Upon our first meeting, I found out that she was a high school biology teacher in San Francisco, 52 years old, a former athlete, lived a few blocks up from my parents, had an addiction to tortilla chips (but who doesn't, right?) and the occasional gin and tonic. She had always been active, doing everything from softball, golf, tennis, rock climbing, basketball, boot camp classes, and running. Eventually, minor aches and pains from all these sports began to turn into more serious injuries and she had to slow down.

During one of the boot camp classes, she tore her right triceps tendon and had to have surgery. Six months later, after basically not doing any activity, she returned to the class but then her elbow "blew up," according to her, and she had to stop yet again. This, along with a total of four knee surgeries throughout her life, a broken foot, low back strain, and a torn quadriceps muscle truly began to take its toll, as you can imagine. The decrease in activity, along with eating foods she knew she shouldn't be eating, and the emotional/psychological stress of not being active, caused her weight to fluctuate to 182 pounds. A trip to her doctor's office, stepping on the scale and having him tell her that she was indeed overweight and in need of lowering her cholesterol levels was the fuel she needed to ignite her fire once again.

As a biology teacher, Rae Ann knew firsthand and taught the importance of proper nutrition and consistent exercise to her students every day. She was also well aware, as I was too, that the human body is not only incredibly fascinating but also amazingly adaptable. Because she had been sedentary by that point for quite some time, her body was craving and in dire need of a new stimulus. That new stimulus was going to be the twice-weekly strength training programs combined with a moderate amount of cardiovascular exercise and a minor change in her mindset regarding nutrition. Mindset? Yes. And here's why.

I previously mentioned that Rae Ann already knew what she needed to be eating,; she just wasn't doing it. I had a strong feeling that once we actually got her moving again, the switch would be flipped and she would be finally listening to her own advice.

It was January of 2010, and Rae Ann weighed in at 177lbs and 34.7% body fat. Her personal goal weight was 140lbs, and together we set a body fat percentage goal of 25-26%. We did not set a timeline. It would take as long as we needed, because I truly believe and still do, that rapid weight loss does not last, and more importantly, it was critical that we designed her program with the other goal of making her functional first, and fit second. The injuries she incurred were still fresh in her mind, and a minor "tweak" could very easily derail her motivation. We stuck to the plan and a year later, she looked like a totally different person and was basically swimming in the sweats I first met her in. She weighed in at 144 lbs. and 25.6% body fat!

Here's how the 52 year-old biology teacher, with a full-time job, hectic commute and a laundry list of injuries finally reclaimed the body she always had. She was simply but subconsciously spending too much time focusing on her injuries and letting them run her life, versus using her years of expertise as a biology teacher to change her habits and get back on track. And guess what? It's ok—we all do it! But Rae Ann reached her "lowest point" and sought out help. Here's how we flipped the switch...

Monday: Spin (20-30 minutes on her own, or a class setting).

Tuesday: Strength training workout "A" w/intervals or a finisher at the end.

Wednesday: Rest day or active recovery (foam roll, mobility, taking a walk, not more than 20 minutes).

Thursday: Strength training workout "B" w/intervals or a finisher at the end.

Friday: REST.

Saturday: Strength training if not able to come in on Thursday, or light cardio (20-30mins max).

Sunday: Strength training workout A or B on her own (if she came in on Saturday to lift weights, she would use Sunday as a long cardio day or mobility, stretching and some light cardio).

This schedule is a sample and was definitely not set in stone. Our main concern and focus was her strength programs, and NOT the cardio. Truthfully, I would have been perfectly happy with only 2-3 workouts per week TOTAL, but Rae Ann enjoyed doing cardio such as spinning and walking and I did not want to take that away from her. In my experience, I've found that if I asked a client to limit certain activities that they truly enjoy doing and replace them with being in the gym for most of their workouts, they lose their motivation. It was crucial for her success to encourage her to do those activities that made her feel good, and I'm glad I made that decision.

Recovery and rest were also key components of her program, and I encouraged her to take time off between strength training sessions. Resistance training breaks down muscle tissue, and it is during the time after a session that the tissue begins to rebuild and recover, hence influencing muscle growth. If she lifted weights two days in a row or more, it could very well be detrimental to her progress. So, easy cardio, mobility work or a complete day off is what was recommended.

I can proudly say that I have learned from the best trainers in the industry. In putting together Rae Ann's program, I used that knowledge and expertise to design her workouts to include the following:

- Dynamic warm-up/movement preparation—exercises that are designed to prepare the body for movements that will be done in the subsequent strength routine. These are typically full body exercises that also increase blood flow to the muscles, as well as core body temperature.

- Core strengthening—generally best when done before the rest of the strength workout. Exercises like planks, hip bridges, cable wood-chops, mountain climbers and farmer's walks are excellent core exercises to incorporate as they target the abdominals, low back extensors, glutes and hip flexors. As a trainer I typically see these exercises being performed at the end of a workout, when the body is already exhausted, rather than at the beginning, when the body is fresh and capable of performing better. Due to Rae Ann's injury history, I wanted to ensure that her core was activated before we began any other compound movements.

- Strength/Resistance Training: I took Rae Ann through nine phases of programs, with each phase lasting 4-6 weeks before we moved on to the next. She always had two separate workouts to do during the week, so as to ensure variety and decrease any chance of boredom! During each session, our goal was to pick 1-2 different exercises to adjust the load on, in order to progress from the previous completion of the same workout. For example, if she did 2 sets of 15 dumbbell bench presses with 15 lb. weights (30 lbs. total), I would have her attempt 2-3 sets with 17.5-20 lb. weights for 10-12 (or 15 if she can push them out) reps on the next workout. Each phase was completely different than the previous one, and she never knew what was in the next phase. We definitely repeated the same movement patterns, but always varied the repetitions and load.

- "Finisher" or Interval/Energy System Training: instead of having her jump on the treadmill or elliptical immediately after our strength training session, we would go through a metabolic challenge at the end. This could entail kettlebell swings, intervals on the rowing machine or spin bike, or jump squats on the TRX (and yes, after strengthening and stabilizing her knees, along with her ankles and low back, she was able to do jump squats!!!).

Below is the first Phase of her program, which includes two separate routines. Pictures and video of these exercises at: www. fitness-evolved.com

PHASE 1/WORKOUT "A"

Dynamic Warm-Up: 6-8 each

1) Squat to stand

2) Inchworms

3) 1/2 Kneeling t-spine rotations

4) Leg swings

5) Walking knee hugs

6) Glute/hip bridges (single-leg and double-leg progressions)

Core: time-based or 12-15 reps

1) Full plank (hold as long as possible)

2) Single leg lowering on bench or Stiff arm pulldowns on cable or with resistance band

Strength:

1a) In-line lunge—1-2x 15 reps

1b) Standing cable mid-row (feet even)—1-2x15reps

2a) Hip/thigh extension—1-2x 15 reps

2b) Lat pulldown or ½ kneeling narrow grip pulldown on cable—1-2x15 reps

3a) High to low wood-chops on cable—1-2x 12-15 reps

3b) Incline bench press—1-2x 15 reps

Finisher: 5-6 rounds of 30 sec high-intensity intervals on the spin bike, with 60-90 seconds recovery between sets.

PHASE 1/WORKOUT "B"

Dynamic Warm-Up: 6-8 each

1) Squat to Stand

2) Inchworms

3) ½ Kneeling t-spine rotations

4) Leg swings

5) Walking knee hugs

6) Glute/Hip bridges

Core: 12-15 reps

1) Cable standing anti-rotation press

2) Medicine ball floor slams

Strength:

1a) Body weight squats or overhead squat w/resistance band for assistance—1-2x 15 reps

1b) Bent over reverse flye (Rae Ann's personal favorite....)

2a) Pull through's on cable (work on hip-hinging)— 1-2x 15 reps

2b) Alternating DB bench press on swiss ball— 1-2x 15 reps

3a) Static Lunge with rear foot elevated—1-2x 12-15 reps

3c) 3 pt DB row—1-2x 15 reps

Finisher: 6-8 rounds of 20-25 second high-intensity intervals on the rower, spin bike, or doing kettlebell swings.

As you can see, Rae Ann's programs consisted of full body movements that targeted her major muscle groups, and in order to be cautious with her knees, we did a good amount of body weight exercises first before adding any load. All of her Phases included the following movements:

Knee dominant (lunges, squats)

Hip dominant (bending from the hips—bridges, step ups, pull through's, deadlifts)

Pushing (chest presses, shoulder presses, and eventually push-ups)

Pulling (rows, lat pull downs, reverse flyes, assisted pull-ups)

Rotational stability (movements that require coordination of the neuromuscular system and transfer of energy from one portion of the body to another through the torso. Exercises such as wood-chops, grappler twists and medicine ball side throws are examples of rotational stability movements.)

In all honesty, there was nothing "magical" about her programs. I made sure she was doing what we call "bang-for-your-buck" exercises, progressing her safely on loading the exercises, and getting enough rest between sets, based on what phase we were doing. What was pretty magical, however, was the first time we both really noticed together how much stronger she looked, and more importantly, how much confidence she was exuding. The first time she walked into the gym wearing workout tights and a tank top blew me away! She had "guns" instead of biceps, her back muscles were on full display every time she knocked out a pull-up, and her midsection was no longer a "jelly-belly," according to her five year-old niece. Rae Ann put in the work, stayed patient, and took care of herself. She listened to my advice, took rest days when needed, and did just enough with her diet to see a positive change in her body.

Working with Rae Ann has proved to me that indeed, we all stumble, sometimes even fall down, and even when the last thing we want to do is lift our head up for fear of embarrassment, we JUST.SIMPLY.HAVE.TO. Our bodies are designed to get better, become stronger, and improve with age, which is far from what we are taught when we're younger. There are constant reminders of "it's all downhill from here!" or "this is just what happens as you get older" being mentioned on television, in magazine articles and even in some health professions. It is truly a shame and completely NOT TRUE. When it came down to her injuries, we did not let them dictate who she was as a person. When that happens, there is very little room for improvement or growth. At 52 years old, this biology teacher made some small changes to her lifestyle that impacted her life in a big way. She finally began to practice what she was teaching all these years, and threw away all those baggy clothes to prove it.

About Carmela

Carmela has always been an athlete. From a very young age, she dabbled in ballet, gymnastics, ice skating, volleyball, and devoted a large amount of her teenage through college years to track and field. While at Willamette University earning her Bachelor's degree in Exercise Science, Carmela truly found her passion with movement, sport, fitness, and rehabilitation. She is a certified personal trainer through the National Academy of Sports Medicine.

Carmela is co-owner of Fitness Evolved in Berkeley, CA with her partner Andy Clower, and she is a Certified Personal Trainer with the National Academy of Sports Medicine. She takes great pride in learning under the tutelage of Alwyn and Rachel Cosgrove of Results Fitness in Santa Clarita, CA, as well as Dr. Eric Cobb of Z-Health Performance Systems in Phoenix, AZ. Lifelong learning is an area that Carmela truly believes in and continues to learn with each new client she meets. She enjoys training and coaching a diverse group of clients but has always been passionate about training female clients, largely due to the fact that as a young female athlete, she was enamored by what her body was capable of accomplishing and was lucky enough to have some amazing coaches. From that point on, she promised to one day be able to do the same thing for someone else.

Fitness Evolved is a health, wellness and performance training facility in Berkeley, CA that strives to create life-long athletes out of its members. The systems and techniques used at Fitness Evolved continue to set their facility apart to become known as the most "cerebral" gym in the San Francisco Bay Area. Their training system helps put clients back in control of their own performance, continually making lasting breakthroughs in areas including pain relief, injury prevention and mindset. They are most often sought out by clients who have "tried everything else" with no results.

Instead of waiting for the mainstream fitness industry to catch up with the latest research, the Fitness Evolved team sought out those who are already applying it well—the world leaders in fitness and performance training—and spent thousands of dollars and countless hours being mentored by and learning from them. For more information about Carmela or Fitness Evolved, go to: www.fitness-evolved.com

CHAPTER 7

WHERE THERE'S A WILL, THERE'S A WEIGH.

BY MIKE WUNSCH

Will's way wasn't working. A former High School Football player now in his forties, he realized he needed a change. With a career working nights, a body that was no longer 18 and no longer exercising 6 days a week for hours at a time, he was losing his athletic appearance, personality and function. He wanted change, so he tried every method he could think of in order to chase how he used to feel. He tried several fad diets that consisted of things such as eating only once a day, drinking only shakes for food, and diet drinks with fast food. You name it, he tried it; and he tried it alone.

Will saw our ad in a local newspaper and decided to come to Results Fitness and we discussed his goals. When I asked him about his goals, he gave the same answers everyone else in the world does: lose fat, add muscle, feel better, look better, and perform better. Tell me something I don't know. That is when I asked him the pivotal question that digs down to the soul of a person.

"What do you mean?" Will asked with a confused look on his face. "What happened?" I asked again with a serious look on my face. "Something happened to you or you wouldn't be here – something ALWAYS happens." I went on to explain to him that over the years and over the thousands and thousands of training sessions I've been fortunate enough to be involved in I learned a valuable lesson about the fitness industry. I learned that there is always an underlying reason people make change. Something happened. We know there are things such as gyms that exist for our well being. We know eating right should be a part of our lives. We know that we should exercise properly. Why don't we? Something hasn't happened…yet.

A doctor may have told them to lose weight for their health. A family member or friend or even a stranger may have made a comment about their appearance. A mirror may have just for that one perfect time at the perfect angle revealed something. A coach may have given reasons as to why you are not on the team. A daughter or son may be getting married. A vacation is coming up. A reunion is coming up. I just got divorced and want to look better for someone. They can't take the pain anymore. No clothes fit anymore. I got hurt. I have to take medication. Any of these sound familiar? If one digs deep enough, there is always something.

For Will, it was simple. He told me that one day he was reading an article on the detrimental effects of Diabetes in African American Men in their forties. As he kept reading down the list, he became literally scared to death. The list was long and serious: kidney failure, blindness, amputation, erectile dysfunction and death – to name just a few. It was enough for him to make a change. He decided to change the future and be proactive about his health. Something happened to him.

When "Something Happens," you have the motivation to do things you normally would not do. That one thing that occurred will get you out of bed when you are tired. You will make better nutritional choices when the right choice is harder than the easy one. You will go to the gym when you would rather stay home. That one thing will give you the strength to do things you normally would not do in social situations. You have a stronger chance of making the right decisions amongst other people during occasions such as eating out.

As a member of the gym, Will competed in a contest that we host at the gym called New Year, New You. He was joined by four other teammates and competed as a team against other teams to see which team lost the most fat. The contest lasted six weeks and by the end of the contest, Will had actually lost more fat than anyone else in the contest and led his team to a solid second place finish. With over 25 pounds of fat lost in six weeks, he certainly finished first in our eyes.

Will attended group classes at Results several times a week for the duration of the contest. He performed three strength-based classes a week and another two metabolic classes per week. He wrote in his food journal every single thing he ate and drank. We kept track of his mood, his energy and sleep, and each week we reviewed it with each other. We noted where he was doing well, and where he needed to change some habits. We measured his body fat at the start of the contest, the middle of the contest and at the end of it. We used this information to track his progress, keep him motivated, and the most important aspect of tracking is that we knew if what we were doing was working or not. We knew he was eating right and not starving himself. We knew that because we tracked his muscle mass along with his fat mass. He was dropping several pounds of fat per week and holding on to precious fat-blasting tissue called muscle. We had hard data to prove what we were doing was working. At that point, it became a fact that what we were doing was working and not just my opinion. The numbers never lie. His fat was down, his mood was up.

The program that Will followed was a strength-based program that was designed to burn calories while promoting muscle gain. We used non-competing muscle groups and compound total body exercises. The program consisted of a self-myofascial release with a LaCross ball and foam roll to prepare the body tissues for the upcoming work. Think of that as self-massage to loosen up the body before it gets worked hard. Next he performed a R.A.M.P, which stands for Range of Motion, Activation, and Movement Preparation. This can be thought of as a "warm up." His RAMP consisted of stretches and exercises that begin very slowly and gradual. The complexity and intensity of the RAMP increased as he performed it. Muscles that are tight are stretched, and muscles that are weak are activated in order to further improve his ability to move.

After his RAMP, he performed paired exercises that were designed to effectively work his core. He performed exercises that transmitted force from his lower body to his upper body and vice versa, and exercises that required him to resist twisting and bending at the spine. Ineffective exercises such as crunches were definitely out of the question; we needed Results!

His two core exercises were Tall Kneeling Kettlebell Halos and Alternating Spiderman's. He had five minutes and performed each exercise for five repetitions. He alternated between the two exercises, resting as needed. The Halo was performed by kneeling two knees, squeezing the abs and glutes and making small circles or halos overhead with the Kettlebell. His core really had to work hard in order to prevent him from twisting and losing his posture and form. His second core exercise, the Spiderman, was performed by assuming a push up position and alternately taking big steps, with his feet trying to step out far enough so that his foot would be close to his hands. He needed great core strength and hip mobility to remain in perfect push up position while stepping.

After the core exercises were completed, he performed two power development exercises. These types of exercises are designed to increase one's ability to generate force. They are tremendous fat-burning exercises and are typically very fun to do. He again had 5-minute time periods and performed each exercise for five repetitions and alternated between the two exercises. The first power exercise was a rollover floor slam. He took a medicine ball and placed it on the floor in between his shoes. He would then very rapidly stand up with the ball as he was going from a squat position to a tall standing position. During the ascent, he would roll the ball out to his side – forming a large arc. This long fast arc would end over his head and he would slam the ball as hard as he could on the floor. Once one side is done, the medicine ball is "rolled" to the other side on the way up.

The second power exercise was a Sandbag clean. The sandbag was placed on the floor on his shoes and he assumed a bent knee position with his hips back and his torso leaning forward with good posture. He then with an aggressive hip extension "jumped" the sandbag from his shoes up to his shoulders.

The resistance portion of the workout was next. This is the bread and butter of fat loss. This is what we refer to as the foundation of fat loss and the most important aspect of fat loss via movement. Muscle tissue is extremely metabolically active. It takes a lot of caloric burn in order to preserve the tissue – whereas fat is very basic and needs very little energy to preserve itself. With this knowledge, we knew we wanted to lose as much fat as possible without losing muscle tissue.

He had a 15-minute time period to perform three resistance exercises for ten repetitions and a stretch as active recovery between the three exercises. The first resistance exercise was the forward lunge. With one Kettlebell in each hand, he started by standing very tall and would take a big step forward with one leg into a lunge and drive off the heel to return to the start. It was important to really focus on posture and his core during this move. One leg was done for all ten repetitions before the other leg worked.

As an active recovery stretch, he did a side lying rib pull. This was performed for two main reasons. One is that it forces a rest period, and two, the rib pull is an excellent way to increase mobility in the mid and upper back. He would lie on his side and assume the tallest position he could. He then brought up the top knee as high as it would go towards his face. He took his top hand and reached down towards his bottom ribs. He was cued to pull his shoulders down away from his ear. In one fluid move, he would try to rotate his shoulder blades to the floor while the hands were helping gently pull the ribs to help the stretch. If he was lying on his left side, his right knee was brought up to his face, his right hand would grab his left ribcage and he would try to rotate his right shoulder blade to the floor.

Next he did a goblet squat. He held a Kettlebell by the horns up to his chest. He would push his hips back and also push his knees out as far to the side as they would go as he squatted down. He kept his heels down and chest up. His hips went just below his knees to get full range of motion. The final resistance exercise was a split stance 3-point row. He assumed a split stance with his right leg forward and right hand on his right knee to support his back. His left hand had the Kettlebell and rowed the Kettlebell up to his side with a strong pull without shrugging. All ten were done on one side then he switched sides.

He finished the workouts with more SMR and recovery shakes. These two processes helped Will recover faster and enable him to work harder the next workout. The SMR helped redistribute the blood back into his body and the post workout shakes provided his body with the tools it needed to rebuild his muscles.

We gave Will nutritional guidelines as well. The following guidelines are our fat loss principles that we have established over the years that have proven to be successful.

1. Eat within 15 minutes of waking and every 2-3 hours.
2. Have a fruit or vegetable at each meal.
3. Have a good quality protein at each meal.
4. Eliminate processed carbs.
5. Use healthy fats and oils freely.
6. Eliminate caloric beverages and drink half your bodyweight in ounces of water.
7. Supplement with a multivitamin and fish oil.
8. Always have a workout shake.
9. Keep a journal.
10. Plan to splurge 10% of the time.

Results Fitness Group Coaching					
Order Mobility, Activation & Movement Prep	**Sets**	**Reps**			
Foam roll/LAX SMR	1				
			New Year, New You		
Order 5 reps each, 5 min period	**Regressions:**				
1a Tall KN KB Halo					
1b Alt spiderman					
5 mi 5 reps each					
2a Rollover floor slams					
2b Sandbag cleans					
15 min 10 reps each					
3a Fwd lunge					
3b Sidelying rib pulls 5 reps each					
3c Goblet squat					
3d Split stance 3 pt row					
					Notes: Check for pain; Regress any station if necessary to accommodate. Adjust number of rounds if needed for new clients.
Finisher: Vary int. time according to class size	**Sets**	**Reps**	**Work**	**Recovery**	
Regeneraton					
SMR, stretch, post workout recovery					

By following our plans, our guidelines, Will lost an impressive 25 pounds of fat in six weeks. He stuck to our plan, and didn't try anything on his own that was not part of the plan. Now the things he hears from his co-workers are things such as: "Dude, what are you doing?" "How do I become a member?" "You've gotten more results in six weeks than I have in 4 years!" "What diet are you on?" (Will replies it is simply a lifestyle change). His friends and co-workers now ask him for advice. His fiancée tells him he needs to buy a whole new wardrobe and she loves how "skinny" he has become. The other gym members congratulate him every time they see him.

When I first met Will, he asked me if I could put him on our wall of fame when he reached his goal. He said it would make him and his family so proud. I told him "Will, that's on you." It was on him. He made the sacrifice, did the hard work and now is reaping the rewards of what he sowed. Now his plaque shines proudly on the wall of fame at the gym.

I asked Will, "Why were you successful?" His answer was simply, "I am very competitive and knew I could do it, I don't like to lose."

Sorry Will, you lost, and you lost a bunch!

About Mike

Mike Wunsch is the Director of Program Design and Training for Results Fitness – voted one of *Men's Health* Top Ten Gyms for several years in a row. He is responsible for getting everyday people into the best shape of their lives in the shortest, safest and most fun time possible. The happiness that Team Results Fitness makes possible and exceptional customer service set it apart in the industry.

Mike has worked with several top name companies such as Nike, Microsoft, MSN, and publications such as *Men's Health, Women's Health, Shape, Men's Fitness,* and *Experience Life Magazine.* He has been a consultant and author for several best-selling books. He also is a presenter for the National Strength and Conditioning Association and Perform Better.

When Mike is not at the gym, he can be found out in the middle of nowhere with his chocolate lab Ace, hunting the country or shooting jumpshots on the court.

Results Fitness also has several products ranging from exercise DVD's to Mentoring Fitness Professionals on how to run a profitable gym. For any information on the RAMP and Metabolic Training contact the gym at:

www.resultsfitnessuniversity.com

Or call: 661-799-7900

CHAPTER 8

POWERFUL MIND, POWERFUL BODY

BY KIAN AMELI

"If I don't deliver tomorrow, they are going to induce labor."

Not necessarily the conversation starter I want to hear when rounding out a morning of training.

"I really think this baby is ready too, this pregnancy has been a lot easier than the last three."

Nina had been training at Momentum Fitness for just around four weeks before she found out that she was pregnant with her fourth child. After a quick visit to the doctor, she told me that she would like to keep going with her training program for as long as she could. After over nine months of training we hit this moment – giving birth to baby number four.

Looking at Nina's story, what we see is the story of every mom who has taken her first step towards reclaiming her body. Throughout each phase of Nina's journey we can pull advice, training tips, and mindset strategies that transcend the nine months of pregnancy.

RECLAIM YOUR BODY, RECLAIM YOUR LIFE

Each phase of Nina's story gives us a glimpse into what is possible, not only in pregnancy, but in how we all approach fitness. Each of the five *Momentum Fit Tips* should give you insight into how you can change your approach to fitness.

Momentum Fit Tip #1 – Challenge the way you measure success

The simple act of moving is one of those basic human rights that a lot of moms don't get to practice a whole lot. In my conversations with Nina over the course of her pregnancy, I got a lot of insight into how difficult it can be to be a mom. As the days progressed we had to find more and more modifications for Nina, since no one program will fit every single person, especially a pregnant woman, we had to really focus in on what her goals were for the pregnancy.

Looking back at when Nina was first beginning to show, she said "Being pregnant and working out changed how I viewed being fit, I was working hard, getting stronger, but every day I was getting bigger and bigger. Doing it like that allowed all the unhealthy views I had of fitness to die."

We weren't allowed to use the normal metrics of success like percent fat lost, scale weight, or inches lost because - and this should go without saying - trying to lose fat while pregnant is just foolish. It made us really think about how we measure success - if there were no scales, or tape measurers, or body fat analyzers how would we measure success?

In Nina's case we had to focus in on factors I would have never even thought to measure - reduced morning sickness, the amount of energy she had across the day, and her change in mindset.
After just a few months pregnancy Nina had an iron resolution to keep training. Nothing would deter her. Sure she would miss a day here or there, but she would always come back and train hard. She would train at 5 am if that's what it took to get in

and train. When I asked her how she could stay so true to the program with three kids, including one with special needs, and one on the way she said, "After my workout, and as I was on the way home, I would sit at the traffic light and say, 'OK, now I can handle whatever the day holds.' Keeping me going and working out regularly helped me get through the day."

When you invest in your body you have to start thinking about how your mindset is affecting everything else that you do. Training consistently is not just about the physical changes. Once you've conquered the gym you can face the day with a much stronger mindset.

Momentum Fit Tip # 2 – No one is going to tell you to do it

After a particularly tough training session, I told Nina that it was ok if she wanted to sleep in - now you have to realize that at this point I knew how to train someone who was pregnant, but didn't realize all the other factors that go into being a mom, let alone a pregnant mom. Factors like: sleeping while pregnant is really hard! Nina told me that she realized, "No one is going to say 'Go workout!' Anything you want, anything that's worth having, you're going to have to bust your ass for."

That stuck with me for a while. I realized that every single member we had coming through our doors had to make the same decision. Each person has to choose to train over everything else on their to-do list: finishing the dinner that wasn't quite done, their shopping list, sleeping, and even spending some time with their kids. You are going to have to fight for it, and sometimes simply arriving at the gym is the victory. Sometimes in the thick of life, you have to tell yourself that, "I'm going to do the one thing that I can do, even if that's only taking my fish oil and a multivitamin." That simple act can be your victory.

In my professional experience I have never, not even once, heard someone tell me they came in to train today because someone else told them to workout. Changing your life and reclaiming your body must be your decision.

<u>Momentum Fit Tip #3</u> – Tap into the motivating factors in your life

As we approached the midway point in Nina's pregnancy, we had to slow things down a little bit, increase rest periods and decrease the amount of work that we were doing. Even on those mornings where I could tell that Nina hadn't slept a whole lot, or that morning sickness did get the best of her, she would still come in and train. Looking back on her journey Nina told me, "As the pregnancy progressed I would just go through the motions, I figured doing something was a lot better than nothing. With all of my other kids running around, the gym was my sane time. When I got home my kids would always ask me, 'Did you workout today mommy?' Before they started their day, I worked out as a part of my day. Then, as if realizing it for the first time, "it's important for them to know that."

Nina, like so many of us, wants the next generation to lead better lives than we have, and part of that is breaking the cycle of unhealthiness that is bleeding into our culture. Even through one of the most traumatic things the human body can undertake (pregnancy is rough!) she recognized that her workouts were more important than her getting into the gym and moving around. The mindset shift she is creating in her children continuously pushes her into the gym on the mornings when giving up is a much easier option.

Working out each day can become much more than achieving a fitness goal, it can be about helping shape the mindset of the next generation… though looking good naked is still pretty important.

In our day-to-day we forget our bigger "why" – our reason for working out and training. Tap into what motivates you and there will be no stopping you, no matter what comes your way. The bottom line is to not stop, to keep going, and, most importantly, never, ever, give up.

Momentum Fit Tip #4 – Recognize the ebb and flow of your life

After telling me that the doctors wanted to induce labor the next day, Nina left the gym looking like she was going to pop. As the hours progressed, everyone at Momentum Fitness, members and staff alike, was obsessed with checking their Facebook pages, looking for pictures of the new baby and... nothing. We all feared the worst until we saw a post the next day: Nina had given birth without being induced, at some ungodly hour. We were all ecstatic, thinking about how amazing it was that someone could come into the gym, knock out a great workout, then give birth less than 20 hours later.

Once the excitement settled down we waited for Nina to return. And waited... And waited. It wasn't until 3 months later that Nina could return to exercise. "I intended to workout sooner, but Abigail didn't sleep through the night for a long time," she said, "The 3 months I had to take off between giving birth and being able to train again was so hard. I felt like I had a chance to keep the baby weight off and I was afraid that I would lose all of the benefits." Once Nina returned, we had to train around post-baby pains, feeding schedules, and the normal day-to-day of raising four kids.

We are all familiar with the concept of a stoplight: Green means go, yellow means slow down, and red means stop. The same principles apply to the conditions we travel through in our fitness journey. There are times in our lives - like right before a trip to some remote island with beautiful beaches - when we have to 'bust ass' and focus on dialed-in nutrition, or what we call *green light* times. *Red light* times are situations where we have to say, "it's a victory if I get one training session in this week, two is gold, because life is demanding more of me than I can give." Think Christmas time. *Yellow light* times in our lives are what we call the "grind," it's where we have to juggle our busy lives with our fitness and nutrition. During the *yellow light* times, we work hard, but this is the grunt work we put in to see great results.

Nina was coming out of a *red light* period straight into a *yellow light*. We recognize this natural ebb and flow of life is when we can be most effective. Have you ever tried to run a red light - or how about stopping at a green light? If you don't properly manage your time and energy during stressful or extremely goal-oriented periods of time, you won't end up with the result you want. Hit the brakes before it's time to wear a swimsuit and you'll be sporting the same belly on the beach. Speed through Christmas trying to hit every workout, doing life as usual, and there's a very high likelihood that you're going to crash.

Start recognizing what each time in your life is telling you, what it's requiring of you, then you can better apply the gas and brakes, and in turn see results faster and without injury.

Momentum Fit Tip #5 - Revel in the amazing things you have done

"When you invest in your body, you have to start thinking about how your mindset is affecting everything else that you do. I realized that I didn't have to wait until I was the exact size I wanted to be to feel pretty or to buy clothes I look good in." – Nina.

This is probably the most important point we have touched on. You are awesome, right now, without any change. Your body is where you happen; there is no place else that you can be or should be. As Nina and I were wrapping up our interview for this book, she said that she had one challenge for anyone reading. The challenge was this:

"Revel in the amazing things that you have done."

When was the last time you can say that you looked back on your past and truly enjoyed all of your accomplishments? If you're like me, it's been a while! Take a moment and to look and see how far you've come. If you're saying to yourself "Well, I haven't really done anything in awhile," I call bull! You've made it this far in a book on exercise, haven't you? That's something to be proud of. Realizing and recognizing your small victories is a massively important step, because in order to see the results you want to see, you have to be comfortable being the pretty girl in the room, or the stud who just walked in the door – developing that mindset is something we can't do for you.

Let me be clear - if you don't own your body, your results, and how you take care of yourself, then no one else will. As William Ernest Henley put it, *"I am the master of my fate; I am the captain of my soul."*

If there is one thing we have found, it is that if you try to change your body without changing your mindset, there is no amount of work that you can do to create lasting change.

YOUR WORKOUT

As with any workout program, consult with a physician first. In addition, if you are pregnant seek the help of someone who specializes in working with pregnant women – this program is most likely not for you.

This is Nina's program when she came back to the gym three months after having a baby.

For more information, visit: www.MomentumFitnessConcord.com/GWTP.

Nina's Program...

RAMP (Warm Up)

Hip Flexor Stretch

Double Leg Hip Bridge

Side lying clam shell

Side Lying Arm Sweep

Pike Single Leg Heel Lifts

Standing Bat Wings

Toe Touch Squat to Stretch

Walking Cross Body Knee Hug

In Line Lunge

Alternating Lateral Squat

Core Training

Weeks 1 and 2 – Do once; Weeks 3 to 4 – Do twice; Weeks 5 to 6 – Do 3 times

Front Plank – 30 to 60 seconds

Stability Ball Stir the Po – Do 12 repetitions

Rest for 60 seconds

Power Development

Weeks 1 and 2 – Do once; Weeks 2 to 4 – Do twice; Weeks 5 to 6 – Do 3 times

Jump Squat or Power Squat – Do 8 Repetitions

Rest for 45 seconds

Resistance Training

Do all the exercises in round 1 before moving on to round 2

Round 1

Week 1– Do once; Weeks 2 to 4 – Do twice; Weeks 5 to 6 – Do 3 times

Goblet Squat – Do 15 repetitions

3 Point Row – Do 15 repetitions each arm

Side Lying Rib Pull – Do 8 repetitions each side

Round 2

Weeks 1 to 2– Do once; Weeks 3 to 4 – Do twice;
Weeks 5 to 6 – Do 3 times

Step Up – Do 15 repetitions each leg

Push-up – Do 15 repetitions

Open 1/2 Kneel with Rotation – Do 8 repetitions each side

Cardio Intervals

Sprints vs. Speed Squats

Weeks 1 to 2– Do 4 times; Weeks 3 to 4 – Do 6 times;
Weeks 5 to 6 – Do 8 times

Sprint for 15 to 40 seconds

Recover for double the amount of time you worked (i.e.,
15 seconds of work, 30 seconds of rest).

Speed Squats for the same amount of time and rest as
the sprint.

About Kian

Kian Ameli, MS, ACE-CPT, is the founder and owner of Momentum Fitness in Northern California, and is known as the fitness coach to go to when you are ready to "reclaim your body." Going through high school as a "chubby kid," his mission became to change his own body, which sparked the desire to change the way the Bay Area does fitness. Named one of the "most influential coaches in Northern California," Kian has been working in the industry since he was 18 and has created training systems that are based on science and produce consistent results.

Kian is driven by his vision: to create a more effective way for busy people to reclaim their bodies. He started Momentum Fitness in 2010 to create a space where both women and men could get away from the "meat market" mentality, and see real world results in record time. For more information on Kian, check out: www.MomentumFitnessConcord.com

CHAPTER 9

CHASING & BREAKING PRs

BY CRAIG RASMUSSEN

What is a PR? A PR is an acronym for a personal record, and this is what Results Fitness client Jeannine Cascadden is all about. Clients come to us for three primary reasons: to look better, to feel better, or to perform better. Jeannine first came to Results Fitness in 2009 after seeing a local write-up on Rachel Cosgrove's book – *The Female Body Breakthrough*. At age 46, her primary reason for joining the gym was to pass the physical performance test to become a reserve police officer for the city of Beverly Hills, where she also works in the crime lab. "I had not had problems with these types of tests fifteen years prior, but I was younger and in better shape back then. Something had to be done." Jeannine's main issue with the test was that she was unable to get over a wall obstacle during a portion of the test due to a lack of strength and she realized that she needed help. At the same time, she was also unhappy with how her body looked. "In October of 2009, I was also getting fed up with my increasing weight, I was on the far side of my size 14 pants and approaching 215 lbs."

Jeannine had been a basketball player in high school and she decided that some supplemental training would be a good idea to improve her game, so she started weight training. She sought out a local trainer and trained regularly for about a year and actually wound up competing in a bodybuilding show while in high school. She soon found that the subjective nature of bodybuilding didn't really hold her interest and she stopped bodybuilding and weight training altogether until she arrived at Results Fitness.

After having children and being in the workforce for several years, Jeannine began participating in martial arts as her physical activity of choice, which she did for several years. Just prior to coming to Results Fitness, Jeannine and her family decided to join a commercial gym, but they quickly became dissatisfied with it. "There was no real support from the staff and all we ever did was run on the treadmills."

Once joining Results Fitness and getting set up with a properly designed training program focused on resistance training, Jeannine participated in our "New Year, New You" contest and then our "Rock Your Jeans" challenge, which provided instant results for her. In her first year at the gym, she completely transformed herself and lost 35 lbs. of pure body fat and went from the far side of a size 14 into a comfortable size 8 pant. She was also easily able to get over the aforementioned wall obstacle and beat several of her male counterparts in the performance test for the police department.

Jeannine spent this first year or so getting some training experience under her belt and building a proper foundation. She then heard some talk about our gym's powerlifting team and this really peaked her interest, as she has always been a naturally competitive person and this appealed to her as a new competitive outlet. For the uninitiated, powerlifting is a competition that involves lifting the maximal amount of weight possible in three different lifts for "only" one repetition. You receive three attempts at each lift, and you will typically shoot for a PR on your final attempt on each of the three different contested lifts. The three contested lifts consist of the squat, the bench press, and the deadlift. The lifts are also performed in this same order in the competition on meet day. Competitors are divided into age and weight classes and compete against those lifters in their same class, as well as for the title of best overall lifter based on bodyweight and total amount of weight lifted. The lifts are judged by a head judge and two side judges who will give you a white light if your lift is good, once it is completed, or a red light if it is not good. You want three white lights! The best combined total of your top squat, bench press, and deadlift is what you are after.

She approached me about the upcoming meet and we decided that Jeannine was properly prepared, and we started her meet preparation training. She took to the specific powerlifting training like a duck to water. She competed with the team in February 2011 at the USAPL California State Powerlifting Championships where she established a state record in her age and weight class. In July 2011, she competed in her second meet where she dropped down a weight class and established a new state and American record. Her progress has been truly amazing considering the fact that she had very little weight training experience prior to her arrival at the gym. She has now become an honest-to-goodness powerlifter and she pursues it as a competitive hobby. Powerlifting has now become the primary focus of her training programs at Results Fitness.

Jeannine typically does two meets per year and she loves everything about the sport. "The people associated with this sport are great and I love the camaraderie. I also really enjoy having very quantifiable goals and objective measures to grade myself rather that relying on the scale as my measure of fitness. As I have gotten stronger, I have gotten leaner. But what really keeps me motivated is always striving to break my personal records."

Jeannine discovered what many have, that the pursuit of performance goals is a very rewarding experience and a great way to achieve body composition goals, which can be a natural by-product of the process. Outlined below is one of Jeannine's earlier 12-week contest training programs that she used to prepare for one of her meets.

Phase 1, Day A

ORDER	EXERCISE	SETS	REPS	TEMPO	REST
Core Training					
1	TRX Body Saws *timed set of slow reps	1-2	*	30-45s	60s
Resistance Training					
2A	Back Squat	2	5	Norm	60s
2B	½ kneel w/ rot.	2	8 ea.	Slow	60s
3	3s Pause Back Sq.	1	5	23X	90s
4A	Bench Press	2	5	Mod	60s
4B	½ Kneeling Ankle Mob.	2	8 ea.	Slow	60s
5A	Seated NG Cable Rows	3-4	10	Mod	60s
5B	One DB SL RDL	2-3	10 ea.	Mod	60s

Phase 1, Day B

ORDER	EXERCISE	SETS	REPS	TEMPO	REST
Core Training					
1	KB Windmills	1-2	5-8 ea	Slow	60s
Resistance Training					
2A	Deadlift	2	5	Norm	60s
2B	Wall Slides	2	10	Slow	60s
3A	2 Board Bench Press	2	5	Mod	60s
3B	Chins	2	5-8	Mod	60s
4A	Low Cable Split Squats	2	10 ea.	Mod	60s
4B	2 Rope Face Pulls	2	12.	Mod	60s
5A	Top of Chin ISO Hold	1	1	20s	n/a

Notes on Phase 1:

- This phase is done 3 days per week alternating each workout 9 (A&B) on non-consecutive days (M,W,F or T, Th, Sat.) for 4 weeks.

- Prior to performing these workouts, Jeannine performed a "RAMP" (range of motion, activation, movement preparation) or dynamic warm up circuit of 8-10 exercises that lasted about 10 minutes.

Phase 2, Day A

ORDER	EXERCISE	SETS	REPS	TEMPO	REST
Core Training					
1	Ab Wheel Roll Outs	1-2	n/a	30-45s	60s
Resistance Training					
2	Back Squat	3	3	Norm	60s
3A	TRX Inverted Rows	4	6-8	Mod	90s
3B	DB Reverse Lunge	3	10 ea.	Mod	90s

Phase 2, Day B

ORDER	EXERCISE	SETS	REPS	TEMPO	REST
Core Training					
1	½ Kneeling Bar Chops	1-2	10 ea.	Slow	60s
Resistance Training					
2A	Bench Press	3	3	Norm	90s
2B	Chins *perform one set of 3 with 6RM between all warm up sets and work sets of 2A	*	3	Mod	90s
3A	DB Bench Press	2-3	8-10	Norm	90s
3B	Supine Face Pulls	2-3	12	Mod	90s
4	3 Point DB Rows	1	20-25	Norm	n/a

Phase 2, Day C

ORDER	EXERCISE	SETS	REPS	TEMPO	REST
Core Training					
1	Hanging Knee Raises	1-2	6-8	Mod	60s
Resistance Training					
2	Deadlift	3	3	Mod	60s
3A	1 Board Bench Press	3	3	Mod	90s
3B	Slideboard SHELC	3	8-10	Slow	90s
4A	One DB SL RDL	2	8 ea.	Mod	30s
4B	Quadruped T/S Ext/Rot.	2	10 ea.	Slow	30s

Notes on Phase 2:

- This phase is done 3 days per week alternating each workout 9 (A,B,C) on non-consecutive days (M,W,F or T, Th, Sat.) for 4 weeks.

- Prior to performing these workouts, Jeannine performed a "RAMP" (range of motion, activation, movement preparation) or dynamic warm up circuit of 8-10 exercises that lasted about 10 minutes.

Phase 3, Day A

ORDER	EXERCISE	SETS	REPS	TEMPO	REST
Core Training					
1	TRX Fall Outs	1-2	10	Slow	60s
Resistance Training					
2	Back Squat	2	2	Norm	60s
3A	Barbell Inverted Rows (pronated grip)	3	10	Mod	90s
3B	RFE Split Squat	3	8 ea.	Mod	90s

Phase 3, Day B

ORDER	EXERCISE	SETS	REPS	TEMPO	REST
Core Training					
3	SA Farmers Walks	1-2	60 yds ea.	n/a	60s
Resistance Training					
1A	Bench Press	2	2	Norm	90s
1B	Chins *Perform one set of 2 with 4RM between all warm up sets and work sets of 1A	*	2	Mod	90s
2A	DB Bench Press	2-3	6-8	Norm	90s
2B	Seated Cable Rows	2-3	8-10	Mod	90s

Phase 3, Day C

ORDER	EXERCISE	SETS	REPS	TEMPO	REST
Core Training					
1	½ Kneeling Bar Lifts	1-2	10 ea.	Slow	60s
Resistance Training					
2	Deadlift	2	2	Mod	60s
3A	TRX SHELC	3	8	Mod	90s
3B	1 Board CG Bench Press	2	2	Mod	90s
4A	Barbell Step Ups	2	6 ea.	Mod	30s
4B	Hip Flexor Stretch	2	10 ea.	Slow	30s

Notes on Phase 3:

- This phase is done 3 days per week alternating each workout 9 (A,B,C) on non-consecutive days (M,W,F or T, Th, Sat.) for 3 weeks.

- Prior to performing these workouts, Jeannine performed a "RAMP" (range of motion, activation, movement preparation) or dynamic warm up circuit of 8-10 exercises that lasted about 10 minutes.

- Meet week is week 12 (week prior to the competition), Jeannine did a light workout where we did the RAMP and did only the squat and the bench press only on that Tuesday (meet was on Saturday). We warmed up and did 3 sets of 3 reps with approximately 70% of her estimated 1 Repetition Maximum.

About Craig

Craig Rasmussen is a program design specialist and performance coach at Results Fitness in Newhall, California. Results Fitness has been named as one of America's top ten gyms by *Men's Health* magazine multiple times.

Craig has been featured in several national publications including *Men's Health*, *Men's Fitness*, *Muscle and Fitness*, and *Runner's World*. He is a competitive powerlifter and Craig also coaches our powerlifting team at Result's Fitness. He is a Certified Strength and Conditioning Specialist through the National Strength and Conditioning Association.

For more information, please visit: www.resultsfitnessuniversity.com.

CHAPTER 10

FITNESS CHANGES LIVES

BY DANIEL JACKOWICZ

I guess you could say my entry into the fitness profession is a fairly common one with some not so common caveats. Growing up, I was always inherently athletic and exceled at sports without too much effort (which was good because I didn't put in anything past the minimum amount anyway), but there was a root problem other than lack of effort and motivation. I was fat. Standing at 6'4" I hid it well, but I was still fat and I always had been, so it was normal.

Senior year of High School, 2004, I remember standing on the scale in pre-season baseball practice and weighed 311 pounds. A week after that on the first day of official practice, I injured my knee, simply running the bases on a hit, which would require two surgeries over the next two years to fix.

During the physical therapy on the second knee surgery, I had a therapist who was a former athlete and very knowledgeable in terms of fitness and athletics, whereas all experience I had previously was based on athletics and sports specific skills, not fitness, lifting or strength and conditioning. She opened up my eyes to general fitness, strength and conditioning as well as the blatant truth that some weight was going to have to come off for the knee to ever be fully recovered.

With that, when I was cleared to do so, I joined a gym. I had no idea what I was doing looking back, but I was in there working hard on the weights, doing too much traditional "cardio"/aerobic training and not eating nearly enough. In less than a year, I went from just over 300 pounds to just above 200 pounds.

Looking back now, I was thin but I didn't look good. The scale was down nearly 100 pounds, I looked like a different person but my body fat was not down in the same proportion in comparison, and any muscle mass I did have under the fat was nonexistent now. I didn't know that I'd become under muscled while still being "skinny fat," just in a smaller size until I saw a picture of me arm wrestling at a family function and my neck and arm look skeletal. You can see that picture at: *www.dannytwoguns.com/ getwiththeprogram.*

When I saw that, it ignited the desire and passion for information in the fitness profession that is still with me today. I knew how to do things the wrong way, and it was time to learn how to do them the right way.

In the following year, I started working at my first gym, met one of my now best friends (Sean) who was a trainer there, and began learning the right way to do things. During that time, I put back on about 40 pounds, lowering my body fat percentage, and increasing my lean muscle mass substantially in the process.

It was also in this time, around 2006, that I first became a certified personal trainer at the insistence of Sean. We'd been lifting together over that year, experimenting with different intensities and training methodologies and sparking my interest to officially get in the field and start helping people in their goals and not have to go through it the wrong way like I had. In reality, simply losing "weight" isn't that challenging, but losing it the right way, while losing the right kind of weight and keeping the right kind of weight offers a substantially higher difficulty.

Growing up, I never knew what I wanted to do for a career. I knew I wanted to help people in some way but never had an outlet to do so until I started training and coaching people in their goals and fat loss journeys. What I wanted to do was becoming clearer, but it still wasn't definitively apparent.

Going through a major transformation changes a person not only physically, but also mentally and emotionally. The transition from insecure, self-conscious fat kid to insecure, self-conscious person two-thirds the size is something you don't hear about too often when people talk about major transformations.

You hear about "how confident they've become" or "how much better they feel in their new body," but realistically any of that comes further down the road. It is taboo to talk about, but the outside world sees and treats you differently when you are 311 pounds and obese and when you are 200-240 pounds and lean and fit. One can say that it isn't the case, but in reality it's true and "it is what it is."

Things never really "clicked" for me personally and for my transformation until one client and her story.

Enter Brandy...

I'd been training clients on and off for almost 5 years before I started training Brandy. There were multiple success stories and great body composition transformations over that time period, but I couldn't relate specifically to them as I did with Brandy, and none of them impacted me as personally – though our stories are a little different.

When I first met Brandy, she always had a smile on her face, but she was shy, insecure and reserved in a way that you could tell wasn't really her, but what she had become accustomed to.

Brandy didn't grow up heavy or overweight. It was only after having her first child that her weight became an issue. The weight that she put on during pregnancy that was normal and temporary became normal, and six years later, she weighed 2 pounds heavier than she did when she delivered.

I'd been trying to get Brandy to start a free trial with me for a couple of months and I never had any luck past money issues or "I'll think about it." I had all but given up trying to convince her and then one day, seemingly random and out of the blue, she came up to me after one of my client's training sessions and said, "Alright, I've heard all of these great things about you and your clients. How do I get started?"

I later found out, the main catalyst wasn't all the great things she'd heard about me, though there were many ☺, it was seeing a picture (weighing over 200 pounds) taken at the MSquerade 2012 charity event that told her she not only needed a change, but she needed help in order to do so. The goal became, that by the time the MSquerade 2013 came around, the picture that resulted would be completely different.

And we did just that. The 2013 MSquerade came around and Brandy was weighing a lean 156 pounds with a completely different body composition and most importantly, a completely different mindset and outlook on life. Plus she had a rather handsome date with her this year...

I've seen clients change significantly physically like Brandy has, but haven't seen them change mentally or emotionally as much, which is where she and I related the most. She changed from shy, insecure and reserved to a strong, capable and most importantly, confident woman who now feels she can voice her opinion and stand up for herself where before she felt like she couldn't. She, like me still struggles with the whole "being a different person" aspect, but the progress she has made in that sense cannot be described in text in a book. Brandy showed me that I'm not in the fitness profession or business, but I'm in the profession of changing people's lives for the better, and that is what makes the difference.

You can see the before and after 2012 and 2013 MSquerade pictures and transformation at: *www.dannytwoguns.com/ getwiththeprogram*. And here is how we made that happen…

Most of the time when a potential client objects because they can't afford your services, it's because they do not value your service and what you can provide enough to justify the money needed. They'd rather spend the money each month on coffee, lunch, clothes or whatever materialism their heart desires. But with Brandy, there were actual monetary limitations we had to work with, so the program we had to work with wasn't the ideal scenario or where I would start most people if the option is there.

In an ideal scenario, I recommend clients do two semi-private sessions and a metabolic group personal training session each week for optimal results. I no longer offer an option like Brandy had when she started out, but the initial first few months was a personalized semi-private session, a group personal training session based around exercises and movement patterns she wasn't doing in her personal session, and a day on her own each week. Again, not the ideal scenario, but being a complete beginner with time and money constraints, we made it work.

In Brandy's initial assessment, she weighed in at 206 pounds. I took her through the Functional Movement Screen as I do with all clients. Here is her breakdown…

Screen	Left	Right	Total
Deep Squat *"Depth, no problem. Stability, poor."*			1
Hurdle Step	1	1	1
In-Line Lunge *"Forward lean, lacks stability."*	2	2	2
Shoulder Mobility	3	3	3
Active Straight Leg Raise	3	3	3
Trunk Stability Push Up			1
Rotary Stability	1	1	1
Total			12

Scoring a 12 on the FMS isn't too bad, but as you can see, the total doesn't tell the story. When you break it down, her two mobility patterns were no limitations (and both significantly more than needed) and where she gets half of her score. But her stability and functional movement patterns needed work, particularly in stabilizing those patterns as the mobility wasn't an issue at all. She was completely symmetrical as well, which is good.

Whenever clients exhibit a lot of mobility during the shoulder mobility and active straight leg raise screens, I break out to a Beighton Assessment, which analyzes hypermobility, or too much range of motion in a given area.

The Beighton Score is broken down many ways, but I break it down to the ability to put palms to the floor with a straight knee, hyperextend the elbow greater than 10 degrees, hyperextend the knee greater than 10 degrees, bend the thumb to the forearm and bend the pinky back beyond 90 degrees. Brandy was positive on all five of those screens. When we see that level of excess mobility, it is imperative that we "own" the correct ranges of motion and highly emphasize stability, particularly in the thoracic spine and hips.

That was the mindset that went into developing the beginning stages of Brandy's programming. The initial goals were to tackle overall stability, while improving the trunk stability push up and rotary stability scores as her priority patterns.

I design my programs in three month "blocks" and evaluate monthly which exercises should be progressed either in weight or a harder variation of that exercise, which need a different exercise altogether and other general progressions.

The first three months, Brandy's off day workout was intended to get her active, sweating and moving, but be something that wouldn't take a whole lot of motivation to do. The answer was incline walking on the treadmill for 30-45 minutes. The majority of people I generally wouldn't have recommended this to, but it was joint friendly, and being out of shape, it got her heart rate up adequately and she could do it on her own without me, so we made do.

For her semi-private session, I wanted to tackle the FMS priorities and build overall stability as best I could, while still getting a metabolic training effect, and meeting her where she was at her ability levels. Our warm up uses the Results Fitness RAMP model – which is range of motion, activation and movement preparation.

Brandy's first three months looked like this…

• Hip Flexor Stretch	30 seconds a side
• Glute Bridge	6 reps w/ 5 second hold
• Side Lying Clam	8 reps per side w/ 2 second hold
• Quadruped T-Spine Extension/Rotation	8 reps per side w/ 2 second hold
• Quadruped Reach, Roll and Lift	6 per side w/ pause at top
• Standing Glute March on Wall	6 reps per leg w/ 5 second hold
• Wall Leg Swing	10 reps per side
• Squat to Stretch	10 reps w/ 2 second hold
• TRX Assisted Split Squat	6 per leg

The workouts ended up looking like this…

Month I – Semi-Private		Month II – Semi-Private		Month III – Semi-Private	
RAMP		RAMP		RAMP	
1A) Band Pallof Press	1–2 x 30 sec ea	1A) Side Plank	1–2 x 30 sec ea	1A) TRX Plank	1–2 x 30 sec
1B) Plank w/Leg Lift	1–2 x 10 ea	1B) One Arm Farmers Walk	1–2 x down + back	1B) Overhead MB Slam	1–2 x 15
				1C) Prowler/Sled Push	1–2 x down and back
2A) Goblet Box Squat	1–3 x 15	2A) DB Straight Leg Deadlift	2–3 x 10	2A) Goblet Squat	3 x 8
2B) Weight Assist Pull Up	1–3 x 15	2B) Incline Push Up Negatives	2–3 x 10	2B) Weight Assist Pull Up	3 x 8
2C) Quadruped Leg Reach	1–3 x 10 ea	2C) Bird Dog	2–3 x 10 ea		
3A) Single Leg Glute Bridge	1–3 x 15	3A) Dowel Assisted Split Squat	2–3 x 10 ea	3A) Split Squat	2–3 x 10–15 ea
3B) TRX Chest Press	1–3 x 15	3B) TRX Inverted Row	2–3 x 10	3B) TRX Inverted Row	2–3 x 15
3C) Mountain Climber	1–3 x 10 ea	3C) Mountain Climber	2–3 x 15 ea	3C) DB Straight Leg Deadlift	2–3 x 15
				3D) Incline Push Up Negatives	2–3 x 15
4) Battle Ropes	3 x 15 sec on 45 sec off	4) Battle Ropes	3 x 30 sec on 45 sec off		

The group personal training session was our "Buns By Twoguns" aka "Booty Bootcamp" session, which entailed the regressions or basic forms of each exercise in a 30-seconds-on/30-seconds-off or 40-seconds-on/20-seconds-off interval circuit. For the first three months, each session for her was a combination of a plank, side plank from the knees, bodyweight squat, TRX-assisted split squats, glute bridges, straight leg deadlifts, tall-kneeling anti-rotation holds, and other basic exercises centered around movement patterns that she wasn't doing in her private session.

Over the months that followed, the workouts focused on progressing Brandy through movement patterns and more difficult exercise variations such as…

- DB Straight Leg Deadlift to KB Deadlift to Trap Bar Deadlift to Deadlift

- Split Squat to Reverse Lunge to Walking Lunge to Rear Foot Elevated Split Squats

- Incline Push Up Negatives to Push Up Negatives to Incline Push Ups to Push Ups

- Weight Assist Pull Up to Band Assist Pull Up to Pull Ups

- TRX Plank to TRX Reverse Crunch to TRX Pike and other advanced core movements

- etc.

Brandy has been working with me now for a little less than 16 months and a look at her current program looks like this...

Workout A		Workout B	
RAMP		RAMP	
1A) Turkish Get Up	1-2 x 2 ea	1A) Valslide Bodysaw + Pike	1-2 x 15
2A) Deadlift	3 x 3	2A) Front Squat	3x5
3A) RFESS	2-3 x 8 ea	3A) Step Up	2-3 x 8 ea
3B) Pull Up	2-3 x 1-2	3B) Push Up	2-3 x 2-3
4A) Unilateral Hip Thrust	2-3 x 15 ea	4A) Valslide SHELC	2-3 x 12-15
4B) Unilateral Cable Chest Press	2-3 x 15 ea	4B) TRX Inverted Row	2-3 x 15

The progress she has made over that time from where she started to where she is now is incredible. In the past few months, Brandy has hit a 185 pound deadlift as well as getting her first dead hang bodyweight pull up among other great performance goals, as well as killing it in the group personal training sessions she participates in.

Seeing how much Brandy has changed as a new person rather than simply a smaller person as I had in the past, gave me a perspective on how I am in the business of changing lives – not just the fitness business – and that is a great privilege to have.

About Daniel

Dan Jackowicz, also known as "Danny Twoguns" is a certified personal trainer, certified functional movement specialist with the FMS and a Level 2 DVRT certified instructor. He is currently the owner of Twoguns Training Systems, which operates a studio space inside of Nautilus Fitness in Erie, Pennsylvania.

Dan grew up in East Rockaway, New York and relocated to northwest Pennsylvania to attend Edinboro University where he graduated with a Bachelor's Degree in Health and Physical Education. He completed his undergraduate curriculum with an internship at Nautilus Fitness and was hired thereafter. After working in a sales position and part-time as one of the facilities personal trainers, he became an independent contractor to run his own business and eventually started renting studio space in the gym as well.

Dan's popularity has increased significantly over the past couple of years, and he has quickly become the go-to fitness expert in the Erie area due to his continued and consistent client success stories and results, as well as his relentless passion for continuing education and learning as much as he can to continually bring clients results. He offers semi-private personal training, athletic development training and group personal training programs.

What truly sets him apart from other fitness professionals in the area is his genuine desire to help people and his clients. In his spare time, he is reading or watching fitness-related or professional development-related material, attending seminars or workshops, and learning in any way he can.

Dan would like to thank his parents Paul and Gail Jackowicz, Edinboro University professor Dr. Shawn Reagan, Alwyn and Rachel Cosgrove as well as the whole Results Fitness team, Sean Cody for getting it all started, and Annette Brinker of Nautilus Fitness for saying, "You're stupid if you don't start training full time here with all that knowledge you have." Without them, this journey would surely not have progressed the way it has and as well as it has.

For more information, feel free to contact him at (814) 459-3033 or visit: www.dannytwoguns.com.

CHAPTER 11

THE EVOLUTION OF THE NEW YOU

BY HELENA DUZENSKI, DAVID DUZENSKI, DANIELLE KANE & BRIAN KANE

The struggle to shed fat and get healthy is shared by many. On the one hand, that's a good thing because it means that there are a lot of people out there who are trying to change their lives for the better. On the other hand, the fact that it is a "struggle" means that many of them are having a tough time achieving their goal. If you, too, are struggling, take heart and read on. The "Magic 7" elements we lay out in this chapter will lead you to success just as they have for many of our members.

We would like to introduce you to Chris, female, aged 47, who was struggling just like you when she first joined Evolution Fitness. Like many of you, Chris is a busy woman with a lot on her plate. She and her husband are raising four beautiful children, one of whom has autism, which can add to the daily challenges of life. Chris had known about Evolution Fitness for a while through a friend who already belonged, but she didn't think she had the ability to work out like we do. She didn't believe in herself. Then came the fateful day she went to the doctor's and stepped on the scale for the first time in over two years. She was 235 lbs., the heaviest she had ever been. Shocked and dismayed by the number that she saw, she signed up later that afternoon.

Although she was still not convinced she had what it took, she was desperate for change.

Now, one year later, Chris weighs 189 lbs. and has a mere 16 lbs. of body fat left to lose in order to have a healthy body composition for a female of her height. Of her 189 lbs., 133.41 lbs. is solid, lean muscle, which is fantastic, and her body fat percentage is 29.8%. (Normal range for females is between 18% and 28%.) Now, rather than just hoping to fit into regular-sized clothes, Chris sees a future where she is one of the "hot moms" with a toned, fit, athletic body. The transformation in both appearance and mindset is remarkable, not to mention how much healthier Chris is on the inside. One of Chris's primary motivations, besides wanting to fit into normal-sized clothes, was to get her health under control. She knew her family couldn't afford for her to get an obesity-related disease. Her children were depending on her to take care of them and they were still very young. When Chris joined Evolution Fitness she wasn't looking for a quick fix. She was looking for a complete lifestyle change.

So, how come Evolution Fitness worked? What was it that helped her to succeed where she hadn't before? Based on both our expertise and our experience, we believe there are 7 elements to successfully making the type of lifestyle change Chris did, and shedding pounds of body fat in the process.

THE MAGIC 7

#1. The Truth Teller / Measurer of Progress
Believe it or not, it's actually pretty easy to not see what you don't want to face. Take Chris, for example. She had been overweight since the birth of her youngest child, but it wasn't until two years later when she stepped on the scale at the doctor's office that she finally faced the truth of where she was. This is an essential component to making any sort of real change. You cannot change that which you refuse to acknowledge. The upside is that once you do, it often spurs you into action, as it did with Chris.

Once you face your truth, you need a way to measure your progress. At Evolution Fitness, our truth teller and measurer of progress are one and the same: the InBody. The InBody is a scale with the capability to analyze body composition. It tells us exactly how many pounds of fat versus pounds of lean muscle mass a given member has. With the InBody, we can track progress and make adjustments along the way as we never could before. As of yet, however, the InBody is not widely available, although we do recommend doing a search in your area to see if you can track one down. If you can't gain access to one, don't worry. There are other ways to track your progress, which we effectively used with our members prior to the InBody. First and foremost, DO NOT use a regular scale to track progress. It can act as your "truth teller" as it did for Chris, but never step on it again. If you are doing things right, you should be gaining lean muscle mass as you lose body fat. A scale that cannot tell you which type of pounds you have lost and which you have gained is useless. A much better indicator of progress is how your clothes fit. We suggest routinely buying clothes that are one to two sizes smaller and periodically trying them on. In conjunction with how your clothes fit, take notice of how you feel. If you feel great and have more energy, it's a pretty accurate indication that you are eating right and recovering properly.

#2. "Dial It In" Nutrition

Proper nutrition is the number one rule for fat loss and is a MUST for a healthy lifestyle. Without it, you will never achieve your goals, no matter how much you work out. You simply can't out-train a bad diet. With nutrition, we advise our members to keep it simple. If you choose the right types of foods and eat often, it's hard to go wrong. When Chris first joined, she had been unsuccessfully trying to follow a popular point-based weight loss plan, but she learned at Evolution Fitness that focusing on food choice and timing worked best for her. Here are some nutrition basics that she and many other members have followed to success:

1. Eat clean, whole foods. Eliminate all processed foods. If you can't hunt it, gather it, or pick it, don't eat it. If you don't recognize the ingredients, it's not real food; it's a food product.

2. Eat a protein, carbohydrate and fat at every meal. Protein is an essential macronutrient when it comes to your body's ability to burn through fat and build muscle. Aim to eat 0.8g – 1g of protein for every pound of body weight. For your carbohydrate intake, stick to mostly vegetables, and some fruit. Starches should be limited to breakfast and the first meal you consume after your post-workout recovery shake. Your fat intake should primarily consist of plant-based, healthy fats. Consuming these with every meal will actually help your body to burn fat as fuel.

3. Eat often and never skip breakfast. We advise members to eat every 2 – 3 hours, roughly six meals a day, and to eat breakfast within 15 minutes of waking. Your post-workout recovery shake counts as a meal on days you work out. Think of your metabolism as a fire. If you starve it of its fuel, wood, it will burn out. If you pile too much wood on at one time, it will snuff out. But, if you consistently feed it small pieces of wood and kindling, it will stay steady and strong.

4. Follow the 90/10 rule, meaning you can splurge 10% of your meals. If you skip a meal, it counts as a splurge.

5. Drink plenty of water, roughly half your body weight in ounces.

6. Take a fish oil and multi-vitamin supplement daily.

7. Drink a post-workout recovery shake within 15 minutes of working out.

Tip: Keep a food journal. The only way to make informed adjustments along the way is if you know exactly what you have been consuming. Plus, it helps with accountability. "I didn't fully realize what I was eating until I wrote it down," Chris told us. "The journal really helped me fine tune my nutrition."

#3. Exercise: Training 101

When Chris first came to us, she had been training 5-6 days per week with little result. At Evolution Fitness, Chris works her individualized program with a fitness coach in a semi-private setting two times per week, and will usually take one of our Metabolic classes each week. Even though she has cut her workouts in half, she is seeing amazing results. Chris's exercise program is a periodized program tailored specifically for her body's current state and movement ability that adjusts to her results every 4 – 6 weeks. The 9-phase program began with very basic bodyweight movements, progressed into dynamic weight lifting complexes, and is culminating in Phases 8 and 9 (where she is right now) with metabolic resistance training. Throughout Chris's phases we have incorporated bodyweight exercises, dumbbells, barbell training, sleds, kettle bells and other various full-body, functional exercise tools. Below is a short list of exercise program basics to help you get started.

1. **Strength Training is #1 For Fat Loss.** It is your BMR, or RMR, (basal or resting metabolic rate) that largely determines how many calories you burn daily. Your lean muscle mass is what determines your BMR. The more lean muscle you have, the higher your BMR, the higher your metabolism. So, prioritize your workouts. If you have only three hours per week to work out, they should all be dedicated to strength training. Anything more should be some type of high-intensity interval training or a combination of both, which is how we design our classes at Evolution Fitness.

2. **Train movements, not muscles.** Our fitness facility is mostly open space. The exercises we utilize in our programming are full-body, functional moves. We don't isolate muscles. And we don't put our members on machines. Instead we use free weights like dumbbells, bar bells, and kettle bells, plus bands, the TRX and more. And, of course, body weight exercises.

3. **Change it up.** The second you start feeling like, "I got this" or "It's getting easier now" or "This is boring," you've stopped getting results and it's time to switch it up. Our members get

a new program every 4 – 6 weeks. Within that time frame, we progressively add more resistance so as to constantly challenge the body.

4. Recover. Most people forget about the other half of training – recovery. Without proper recovery, you will not see results. It is the stress of the workout that primes the muscle to re-build, but only in recovery mode does it actually do so. Recovery begins with your post-workout recovery shake, but continues with proper rest, good sleep hygiene, adequate water consumption, proper nutrition, and regular stress reduction through meditation, deep breathing, or massage, for example.

#4. Set Goals & Persist

Every expert under the sun recommends setting goals because without them, success is practically impossible. We are no different. You MUST set a goal for yourself and map out a plan of how to get there. We advise setting goals that are attainable (while still allowing yourself to dream big) with measurable markers along the way. It's a good idea is to reward yourself for making progress as you reach certain milestones, such as buying yourself a new dress or treating yourself to a spa day. Once you've achieved your goal, set a new one. Never allow yourself to get complacent. Always strive for new heights.

We have come to understand there is a second, often over-looked, component to goal setting and that is the persistence it takes to achieve them. As Chris can attest to, changing lifestyle habits is a challenge. It is almost guaranteed that you will encounter difficulties and setbacks. Remember, there never lived a success story without some obstacles along the way. PERSIST. When you stumble or fall, pick yourself up as quickly as you can, dust yourself off, and forge ahead. Never, never, never give up and you will succeed.

#5. A Success Mindset

You've heard this before, but we'll say it again. YOU CREATE YOUR REALITY. Yes, you have that much power. This is not some foo-foo, new age concept to be overlooked. It is as real as the nose on your face. How you think and how you perceive your world directly affects your behaviors and actions, which, in turn, directly affect and influence your world, which then acts upon you and directly affects and influences your thoughts and perceptions. And around and around we go. You control two portions of that loop: your thoughts/perceptions and your actions/behaviors. These are what you must focus on wiring for success. Some success mindset basics:

1. Turn your ANTs (automatic negative thoughts) into APTs (automatic positive thoughts). If you find yourself in a negative mind loop, first take a step back and simply observe the thought. Then, release it. It's futile to tell yourself to stop thinking a particular thought, so don't attempt it. If we told you right now, "Don't think about a purple shoe," all you'll be able to think about is a purple shoe! It's not until you focus your mind on something else, on a red shoe, for instance, that you can change the thought in your head.

2. "I CAN" and "I WILL" only. "I can't" is no longer part of your vocabulary. Those words don't exist in a success mindset. If you are having a hard time believing that you can, try starting with "I can't now, but I will soon."

3. No negative self-talk allowed. Speak to yourself as you would your child, your best friend, your mother.

4. Focus on seeing opportunities rather than obstacles. For example, if you are someone with a very packed schedule, you could think to yourself, "I'll never be able to squeeze a workout in. I've got too much going on." Or you could think, "My packed schedule will drive me to be disciplined about getting my workout done first thing in the morning."

5. Do it anyway. When Chris first joined, she was scared to take any of our classes because she didn't think she was

athletic or fit enough. We convinced her to give it a try and, even though she was very afraid, she did it anyway. If you can't get yourself to quite believe, do it anyway. Jump and the net will appear.

#6. Build a Fitness Family

At Evolution Fitness, there are no individual training sessions. Groups only, both large and small. This is because we understand so well the importance of this sixth element. We take care to foster an "in it together, as a team" culture and community. It is one of our core values. Our members love coming to Evolution Fitness not only because they get great results, but also because of the positive, motivational, and social aspect of our fitness facility. We call our fitness family TEAM EVOLUTION and it is a huge part of our gym culture. Many of our members joke that we are the modern-day, healthy Cheers, "where everybody knows your name, and they're always glad you came." This type of environment helps create lasting success. Your fitness family can begin with just one person, a friend or family member who is "in it" with you. From there, you can build and expand. When fitness and a healthy lifestyle are connected with relationships and having fun, they last.

#7. The X-Factor – YOU

Ultimately, it is your willingness, openness, and readiness to change that makes the other six elements work. If you give it your all and commit to the process, then success will be yours. If not, it will always elude you. It's like all the other elements in the Magic 7 build a really, really fast car, but it is only YOU, the driver, who can put the pedal to the metal.

So, there you have it. Those are the Magic 7 elements to a new, healthier, more fit YOU. As Chris will tell you, one of the best things about successfully making this type of lifestyle change is that it has a ripple effect on all areas of your life. Overall, Chris is happier, more balanced, more confident, and better equipped to handle stress. She feels it has helped her to be a better mother too. What surprised Chris most was how easy it was to bring the rest of her family along with her. "One of the best lessons I have learned through this whole process is how much your children model your behavior," she said. "I am amazed that they want to eat what mommy is eating. Going into it, I anticipated a struggle to get them to eat healthier, but it has been surprisingly easy. I see the changes I have made echo in their behaviors and attitudes and I am excited to continue to be a healthy role model for them."

We hope this chapter and Chris's story has inspired you to embark on your own fitness journey and to believe in yourself and your ability to succeed. All it takes is these 7 ingredients to make the change you wish to see. We have a saying we use so often at Evolution Fitness, it has become our tag line: Change Is Now. So, get up, right now, and do something to move you closer to your goal. Maybe in this moment that means joining a gym, or finding an InBody or some other way to face your truth, or going through your pantry and throwing out all the foods that are bad for you. Whatever it is, do it now because change happens right now, in this very moment. CHANGE IS NOW!

Helena Duzenski

David Duzenski

Brian Kane

Danielle Kane

About Helena, David, Brian and Danielle

Helena Duzenski, Co-Owner / Director of Marketing & Communications

David Duzenski, ACE, YFS, Co-Owner / Director of Membership, Fitness Coach

Brian Kane, ATC, CSCS, YFS, SFMA, SFMS, Co-Owner / Director of Program Design, Fitness Coach

Danielle Kane, Co-Owner / Director of Business Operations, Fitness Coach

Evolution Fitness was born of four friends' passion to change the way fitness was done. With the growing number of people trying to get healthy and change their lives for the better, co-owners Brian, David, Danielle and Helena could see the need for results-oriented, solution-based, lifelong fitness. They knew that the only way to really help people change their lifestyle long-term was to provide them with the same type of scientifically-based, individualized exercise program design, motivational coaching, and commitment that is usually reserved for the elite athlete. They understood that while most of their members would never get paid a single dime for anything they did in the athletic realm, they nonetheless were deeply impacted by the health of their bodies and therefore deserved the same thought and care.

Every member of Evolution Fitness is taken through an extensive assessment called the Body Blueprint, which informs the program design department about each member's specific body and movements, assessing their stability and mobility, their imbalances and weaknesses, and overall risk of injury. This data is used to develop individualized exercise programs that get results quickly, effectively, and safely. Evolution Fitness makes it a priority to take care of their members' bodies so that they can enjoy a fit, healthy lifestyle for as long as possible.

David, Brian, Helena and Danielle also recognize that exercise is as athletic as any sport and, in order to get results, their members must push their bodies to new limits and do more than they think they can. That's why positive motivation is a core value at Evolution Fitness and has become a big part of what they are known for. The four friends and business partners take care to foster a team culture and "in it together" atmosphere at their gym so that the members themselves cheer each other on and support one another. This has proven to be an invaluable part of helping their members' achieve their goals.

Evolution Fitness sets itself apart by providing the same quality program design and positive, motivational coaching reserved for the elite athlete to all of its members. But, none of that would mean anything if it wasn't also a fun place to work out. Danielle, Helena, Brian and David recognize that unlike the elite athlete, their members neither have the desire nor the time to dedicate themselves solely to their bodies and performance. For most of us, working out only becomes sustainable when it is a fun, shared experience. The coaches and staff at Evolution Fitness strive to make every workout and every experience at their gym a pleasurable one. The team mentality and culture at Evolution Fitness lends itself to a fun, social atmosphere where lasting relationships are formed and each member feels part of a larger community – their fitness family which they call Team Evolution.

Helena, David, Danielle, and Brian are proud of what they have accomplished so far and look forward to continue to evolve fitness, and Evolution Fitness, to the next level.

To learn more about Evolution Fitness, visit: www.EvolutionFitnessNow.com or call (856) 751-1300.

CHAPTER 12

WHEN DISCIPLINE AND WILLPOWER ARE OVERRATED, AND DESIRE AND KNOWLEDGE ARE NOT ENOUGH

BY HRISTO HRISTOV

I have spent 20 years as a competitive athlete. Over the last seven years, I have been a health and body transformation coach. Throughout this process I have learned many lessons in life. This would have taken many years had I chosen a path pursuing other interests.

Discipline, willpower, knowledge, and desire are NOT the keys to success in your health and fitness. What is the ingredient to success?

My father played soccer professionally. I am not sure if my love and passion for soccer came from him or just the culture of my upbringing. Regardless, I developed a commitment, drive, and willingness to sacrifice in order to be a professional soccer player. I remember training up to three times a day. There were countless trips to the local stadium where I would do sprints, jumps, and lifting weights. I will never forget the excessive heat of those hot summer days. At night, the return trips to the stadium for sprinting, and running stairs with cuffs filled with sand around my ankles to make it more challenging.

My desire to be a pro was intense. I even remember crying in the bathroom about the possibility of me not becoming a professional soccer player. I was consumed with my goal. Life did not exist beyond soccer. Later, I joined the youth soccer team in my home town of Petrich, Bulgaria. I did not have any idea of what it took to become a pro. I was very young and driven.

The physical environment was not optimal. The field where we played was dirt and filled with holes. The soccer balls were old and ripped. The coaching was not going to help me make it to the next level. Nevertheless, I kept on pushing forward. I had the desire and the passion. My skills improved and I began to get better than some of my teammates who were more talented than I was. I was playing better than many of them during practices. However, I did not have the necessary game experience to propel me beyond their level. I became frustrated because I believed that my work ethic would get me to the next level. But when they played me for a brief time in a real game I felt pressured to perform (because if I did not I was afraid that my coach was not going to play me again), combined with not having experience in the right environment, I performed below my potential. I came to the conclusion that I needed game experience. The "real" game is completely different than just a scrimmage or practice. The environment and dynamics are different. Thus, I learned that being in the right environment is a vital component to success. My dream to be a pro soccer playing was slipping away.

I came to the US without knowing any English. I even remember running on the street and people passing me by were greeting me by saying: "How is it going?" "How are you doing?" and I was smiling not knowing what any of it meant. A few years later, I was working out at a local gym, observing the personal trainers training people, and helping them improve their health and fitness. I became intrigued and started asking questions about the profession. I soon made a decision to follow a new path.

Thus, I became a certified personal trainer.

My passion for health and fitness immensely increased the more I learned about the topic. I also fell in love with nutrition, and its effects on our health, performance and body composition. I kept devouring all of the information I could find on fitness and nutrition. I was determined to learn as much as possible. My goal became to equip people with the ability to achieve the health and body that they desired. Knowledge was very useful in accomplishing desirable results. However, I realized that something was missing. My clients did not have the complete picture. I knew how to apply it to myself. My clients were not achieving long-term results. They knew what to do and what was healthy. I was being paid but I was not happy with the overall results. I came to the realization that knowing what to do is not enough.

People invest time, energy, and resources to health and weight loss. They are self-conscious about their image. My clients knew what to do. Yet they lacked the commitment to stay focused long-term. I became consumed with learning more about my clients. I needed to learn more about whom they are, how they think, what are their goals, motivations, and values. I had to invest in my clients. They invest in me. I knew that proper communication would be integral in helping people bring all of these points together. My clients had to come to a deeper awareness and tap into why they should be exercising and eating right.

They wanted to do the right things. My clients desired health and fitness. However, they lacked the commitment to remain focused on their goals. I was getting some common excuses for my client's and my failures:

They	Me
Well, I love chocolate a lot	Well, I love chocolate too
I love food too much	I am glad you do, you would be dead if you did not

I don't have discipline	Do you have the discipline to wake up early and go to work every day?
I don't have motivation	Do you have the motivation to take your kids to sports and activities?
I don't have time	Do you have time to go to work every day even when you don't feel like it?

They were motivated and disciplined to do certain things but not others. I wanted them to put the pieces together themselves and reach the "aha" moment. It was not so much about discipline, time, motivation, energy, etc., it was about finding the missing link…the "reason why."

It was not simple. I learned that being the fitness expert and teaching people how to exercise was not going to give them the whole picture. In order for me to help them in the long-term, I needed to be an effective coach. I needed to be able to pull them out of plateaus. Many were unaware of how to remove themselves from their path to failure. I had to lead them to places where they could discover how to be successful. I needed to be able to help them tap into a deeper meaning in their lives. Just losing weight and looking good is not a long term solution. I was not going to be able to do that just by showing them how to exercise and eat. A trainer cannot do that, only a coach could lead them in a transformational way.

I started working to become an effective communicator. I focused on leading people. I love learning. It was a fun and challenging journey. My confusion began fading away. I started to form a clear picture on how things work. My clients began starting slowly to take action on tasks they were resisting previously.

It became evident that the reason my clients were not succeeding in seeing the long term results was due to my lack of communication and investment in them. I took full responsibility. Every time I felt like blaming them or their situation, I caught myself and redirected my thoughts to: "What can I do differently for them to move closer to their desired goals?" This kept me focused on finding new ways of exploring and attempting different options. I could easily have blamed it on them or the circumstances. However, that assumes that it is somebody or the fault of something else. It closes my opportunity to help them solve their problems.

My journey of failing to achieve my dream to be a pro soccer player along with my initial training experiences have led me to the following conclusion: Knowing what to do, having the desire, and willpower are not enough.

So if discipline and knowledge are not the main factors for a lasting change in health and fitness, what is it?

Well, we know the old saying: "working smart, not hard is the answer." This saying has a lot of truth. If you have a difficult time changing your behavior, there are three things to do in order to make a lasting change whether it is exercising or eating right.

DIRECTION, FEELING, AND ENVIRONMENT.

After we get to know the person's personality, goals, and where they are now, we can start implementing those three steps. Let's use an example. Let's say you want to lose 35 lbs. of fat, or you are already thin but you lack energy and have bad habits for not eating well and not exercising.

1. Direction. Too often people are focusing on the big picture, and that scares them, which automatically tells the brain that they can't reach their goal because it is too much and too far away. Don't think big picture, think in terms of specific behavior. Don't be ambiguous, give yourself specific, clear steps you can take to start on the path of change – for example, if you currently eat two portions of daily vegetables, increase it to three. Don't change anything else for two weeks. Then move on to another small behavior. The smaller and clearer the step the better – this is vital.

2. **Feeling.** Knowing something isn't enough to cause change, it is the emotions and motivation. People that smoke know they should not, but they do it regardless. You need to tap into the feeling, motivation and the reason why you should lose weight. Don't choose to exercise because you know it is the right thing to do. You won't tap into the intense feeling and motivation that way. Find something that makes your heart race, something that motivates you to act. If you search for it you will find it. Maybe for you it is very important lose weight because you really value keeping up with your grandchildren. Perhaps you want your children to grow up in a healthy family and you have realized that the only way for this to happen is by you serving as an example. Whatever it is, find the intense feeling. The word intense is the key.

3. **Shape The Environment**. External environment plays a big role in lasting change. When the situation changes, the behavior changes. If you find yourself trapped in one place with your fitness improvement, take a look at the environment. Is the surrounding environment supportive? Are the people around you fully supporting you with your journey? When you are trying to improve healthy eating habits, do you have your fridge and pantry equipped with foods that will help you do that? Do you associate with friends and family that are on the same page with you? Do you have a gym membership and never go? Is there support and direction at the gym? Do you see much improvement? If the answer to any of these is no, change that environment. Hire someone that will coach and keep you accountable.

Now you know more about what it takes to have lasting success with your health and fitness than 90% of people. But as you already know, knowledge is only potential power. If not applied, it is worthless. Now pause for 20 seconds and ask yourself the question: "What is my next step going to be?"

Key quotes for change in behavior:

"The Great Wall of China was built hundreds of years ago, hand by hand, one brick at the time. Your life is not as difficult as you make it out to be. Build your life one brick at the time."

"Change isn't an event; it's a process."

"The more you're exposed to something, the more you like it."

"When you set small, visible goals, and you achieve them, you start to get it into your head that you can succeed."

"Self-control is an exhaustible resource. The bigger the change you're contemplating, the more it will sap your self-control."

"Knowledge does not change behavior."

"In almost all successful change efforts, the sequence of change is not ANALYZE-THINK-CHANGE, but rather SEE-FEEL-CHANGE."

"A business cliché commands us to "raise the bar." But that's exactly wrong … you need to lower the bar."

"When you improve a little each day, eventually big things occur…. Don't look for the quick, big improvement. Seek the small improvement one day at a time. That's the only way it happens – and when it happens, it lasts."

"Real change, the kind that sticks, is often three steps forward and two steps back."

"People will persevere only if they perceive falling down as *learning* rather than *failing*."

Special thanks to: my mother Vassi, brother Boris, Blake and our operational manager Julianne for their endless support and patience. I would not be where I am without them.

Reference reading material:

1. *Think and Grow Rich* by Napoleon Hill.

2. *Coach Wooden's Leadership Game Plan For Success* by John Wooden.

3. *Crucial Conversations: Tools for Talking When Stakes Are High* by Joseph Grenny and Ron McMillan.

4. *Switch: How To Change Things When Change Is Hard* by Dan and Chip Heat.

About Hristo

Hristo Hristov is owner of Higher Level Fitness. He is a Best-Selling author, Wellness Body and Life Transformation coach and, as they call him, "a learning machine." His journey started as a competitive soccer player back in Europe in his native country Bulgaria, and evolved as fascination and curiosity about how the human body and mind work and the effects of nutrition on the body. Soon after this discovery, the only logical step for him was to decide to turn it into his profession.

And now, along with his team at HLF, he is focusing on his clients to bring more value into their lives with cutting edge tools, strategies and coaching through his Three Pillar System in Wellness approach: 1. Complexity Conditioning, 2. Premium Nutritional Fuel, and 3. The Mental Edge.

People see the word wellness everywhere. Even the traditional medical community is wearing out the wellness slogans. But the shocking truth is, the key to fitness and wellness cannot be found at the local outpatient clinic, drug store or gym.

FEW PEOPLE EVER ACHIEVE TRUE WELLNESS. His mission is to change that.

He is sharing with you his unique approach, which is proven to produce fast and dramatic results. Three Pillars of Higher Level Wellness consists of:

1. Complexity Conditioning. A custom-designed orchestration of movements that engage muscle systems for optimum fitness conditioning. This works faster and delivers more results than any machine or repetitive workout.

The human body is an interlinked series of bones, muscles, joints, nerves, and ligaments, which are responsible for all movement. This link is termed the kinetic chain and each must work together to produce force. When one link is working inefficiently, it affects the others and can gradually lead to muscle imbalances and injury. His system not only prevents that but also takes your fitness to a higher level.

2. Premium Nutritional Fuel. The right combination of what to eat, when to eat, and how to include essential supplementation to achieve your goals. This is often weight loss, but overall vitality is revved up as well.

3. The Mental Edge. Learn the secrets athletes use to gain powerful advantage in the mental aspect of your game. Your life becomes a series of wins. It's waiting there inside. The fit and fabulous body. The sharp, quick mind. The soaring spirit that elevates life to a higher level.

To learn more about Hristo, go to: www.unleashedwellness.com/

CHAPTER 13

CONQUERING THE FAT LOSS NEMESIS: REPRO-GRAMMING YOUR BODY WEIGHT "SET POINT"

BY PAMELA ALTSTATT, MS, CEP

Please allow me to introduce my personal nemesis to you. Its name is One-Fifty-Three. It is unhealthy, sneaky, and pure evil to me. One-Fifty-Three has snuck up and tortured me three times in my adult life, and I am well aware of it continuously plotting to take over my body again the moment I let my guard down.

The dreaded 153 is body weight in pounds and is my personal bodyweight "set point." It tortures my 5'8" small frame athletic body, which is actually the happiest, leanest, strongest, and functions the healthiest at 135-140 pounds. My dreaded body weight is technically identified as a completely acceptable "normal" weight range for my height. What other people don't see under my clothing is the dreaded muffin-top nor how uncomfortable I am in my clothing. I refuse to buy larger clothes and give One-Fifty-Three more potential real estate. They also do not see my personal disappointment in how I neglected my health during unexpected life struggles. (Yes, I threw my hands up and gave up on my well-being temporarily a few times to mourn the loss of several loved ones as well as to battle numerous hospitalizations from pneumonia as a result of a house fire.) The prescribed high-dose corticosteroids and medications destroyed my immune system and adrenal glands, resulting in depression. The memory of all of these physical/mental set-backs, struggles, thoughts, feelings, and disappointment in myself would rise again to haunt me when I would suddenly realize 153 had silently snuck in my door (body) and took up residence in my stomach area once again. And once I hit my mid-40's, 153 surprised me with his little sister, "5 pounds extra!" Nooooo! Why 153? Why? Oh how I loathe you!

Many of you are nodding your head right now and are relating to that which I've personally shared with you. In fact, your personal body weight nemesis' name happens to be (<u>fill in the blank</u>) and you are just as tired as I am of it haunting you. I am so happy to tell you that you CAN reprogram your body weight set point and rid yourself of this monster permanently!

I am and have been the owner and program director for Upstate Adventure Boot Camp in South Carolina for the past 6 years. Each month I coach 75-125 women and men of all ages who successfully lose 8-24 pounds of excess body fat per month while reversing disease processes.

Several of my clients have lost 80-100 pounds in the past 7-10 months alone. They are getting completely off of and/or their doctors are reducing their medications by 50% for Type 2 diabetes, hypertension, hypercholesterolemia, and depression after only one 4-week camp. I would like to share some incredible and proven fat loss techniques we use that will help to reprogram your personal body weight set point and rid yourself of your body weight nemesis for your life-time.

When you are cold, your brain will send you signals to turn up the heat or put on a jacket. When you are hot it will send signals to turn on the air conditioning or to drink a glass of cold water. Just as your body temperature is programmed to stay around

98.6 degrees, your body weight is naturally regulated to stay within a range of 10%-20% according to the Center for Weight and Eating Disorders at the University of Pennsylvania Medical School. This programmed "set point" is the number on the scale your weight range normally hovers around.

For over 50 years, scientists have debated whether or not the brain (hypothalamus) is attempting to maintain some kind of set level by using a complex set of hormones, chemicals, and hunger signals to adjust appetite, behavior, movement, etc., in order to maintain this set point. One research study showed that when people went on a diet, the amount of circulating ghrelin, a hormone released by stomach cells that acts on the brain to make people hungry, increased. So scientists have discovered that this body weight/body fat set point is not as much about genetics as it is about eating and exercise habits. Over the years your personal set point will increase when consuming too many daily calories and not exercising enough.

If you are over 30, muscle is lost every year so it's easy to see how increased body weight becomes an increasing problem as we age. When you try to lose weight by crash dieting, hormones will spike, sending signals of urges to binge as your body tries to defend its comfortable range.

Healthy eating and changing your exercise behavior has been shown to lower your set point. "When you reach a new set point from a long-term change in lifestyle, the body wants to stay there," says Tsu-shuen Tsao, PhD, an assistant professor of biochemistry and molecular biophysics at the Albert Einstein College of Medicine in New York, who studies energy expenditure. The key to resetting your set point is to lose about 10% of your body weight and then maintain that weight for 3-6 months. This is not the fastest weight loss plan but it is much more likely to result in permanent weight loss.

I understand that when many of you begin losing body fat consistently and significantly, you prefer to continue losing until you reach your goal. That is fine, but you MUST remember that it is imperative that you stay within 10-20% of that goal for a minimum of 12 months in order to change your body weight set point. Otherwise; after a momentary enjoyment of your success, you will find that your body will rapidly return to its previous weight and bring a bigger problem with it…extra weight gain over what you were before you lost the weight! This is why it is imperative that you permanently alter your behaviors to make the healthy changes and weight loss permanent.

THREE PROVEN STRATEGIES FOR CONSISTENT AND SIGNIFICANT FAT LOSS:

1."You cannot out-exercise a lousy diet."

Only 9% of people in the United States can accurately estimate the number of calories they should eat in a day and keep track of their daily food choices. Research shows that people who keep a food journal lose twice as much weight as those who don't. Robyn Flipse, a registered dietitian who has worked with thousands of people to help them lose weight says, "keeping track is the crux of controlling your weight gain or weight loss."

Every client who attends Upstate Adventure Boot Camp specifically for fat loss MUST turn in a weekly food log to me every Wednesday. This is essential for significant and consistent fat loss. Those who do not turn in a food log end up regretting it as they do not lose excess body fat or discover that they actually gained weight. "If you bite it, you write it." Our clients use free programs available at: www.MyFitnessPal.com and www.LiveStrong.com with great success.

Stop with the fad diets! They are causing you more grief and increasing the possibility of you quickly returning to and/or increasing your set point weight. Your family must be able to eat and drink everything as you do for this to be a healthy permanent lifestyle change. If you are eating differently than the others in your home, then you are participating in another fad diet. I highly recommend that you learn to substitute common foods that are increasing your blood sugar and fat storage with foods that keep your blood sugar steady, increase fat loss, and reverse disease processes. Learn more about the benefits of this wonderful way for your entire family to eat for maximum health at: www.gilisting.com/easy-gi-diet/2006/07/low-gi-diet-plan. html

Women should get at least 25 grams and most men 38 grams each day of fiber, according to the Institute of Medicine's Dietary Reference Intake. Tufts University researcher and professor of nutrition Susan Roberts, PhD, has shown that people who eat 35 to 45 grams of fiber a day are less hungry when losing weight and lose more weight than people who eat less fiber.

Maintaining a low sodium diet is also an important aspect of healthy living. As a standard, your dietary intake of sodium should not exceed 2200 mg per day. A healthy range to strive for is 1500-2000 mg/day. Any excess amount can inhibit the absorption of other nutrients and disrupt normal functions of your body. Eating too many salty foods can result in high blood pressure, ventricular hypertrophy and heart failure, osteoporosis and poor bone development, kidney stones and renal failure, dehydration and edema, breathing difficulties, duodenal and gastric ulcers/cancer, as well as electrolyte and hormonal imbalances.

I tell my clients, "If the food you are about to eat can sit on a shelf for a long time, then it is going to sit on YOUR shelf for a long time. Consume plenty of fresh vegetables, fruits, whole grains and lean meats, while completely avoiding refined sugar, processed foods, refined carbohydrates (white bread). Eating a diet that has a high nutrient density will help any sustainable fat loss strategy.

2. Move it, move it!

There is an inexpensive gadget known as a pedometer that counts the number of steps you take each day. The device is clipped to the waistband of your clothing and as your body moves with each step, the counter displays your progress. Studies have shown that weight loss was significantly increased in those who used pedometers compared to those without them. Experts recommend taking 10,000 steps per day to maintain general health and reverse disease processes. For weight loss, the goal should be 12,000 to 15,000 steps for 5 days of each week. Less than 10,000 steps per day will reduce stress but will not result in significant reductions of body fat, body weight, or disease processes. You can add steps by parking farther from the store or your office, taking stairs instead of elevators, and walking while waiting on a child to finish sports activities. I highly recommend the Omron HJ-112, which is available on Amazon.com. The cost is around $22.00. It tracks your step progress for 7 consecutive days, is highly accurate, and will last you for years. You must get one of these. It truly is like having a personal trainer on your hip to keep you accountable in moving your body more each day and within the levels needed for fat loss.

According to the International Journal of Obesity, steady state cardio improves cardiovascular fitness but does not result in significant loss of excess body fat. The study results showed that high-intensity intermittent training (HITT), which is a fancy name for sprints, resulted in very significant reductions in total body fat, subcutaneous leg and trunk fat, and insulin resistance. HIIT can be done on a track, on a stationary bicycle, using weight-training circuits, or any other way that allows sufficient intensity. It is the key is to achieve maximal exertion for several brief periods, separated by rest. This type of exercise is not about burning calories through exertion, but through increasing hormone sensitivity using an intense, brief stressor (hormesis). The study showed that even a ridiculously short period of time spent training HITT each week can result in significant fat loss, despite no change in diet or calorie intake. Please incorporate HITT into your new lifestyle three times per week on non-consecutive days while continuing to do 30 minutes of strength training three days a week. (Kettlebells are an incredible tool for rapid fat loss and increased strength.)

3. Hire an accountability partner

I have very seldom seen anyone having success staying with a program when they've rallied their best friend, neighbor, or friend to "do the program with them." Hire an accountability partner who is more knowledgeable than you. I was in California last year meeting with over 40 of the top fitness trainers in the world. Our business mentor asked our group, "Who in here believes that every person should hire a personal trainer at some time to increase their results?" Of course, we all raised our hand. Then he said, "If you believe it is important, then who is yours?" Several months later, I was talking to a friend of mine to schedule a visit. This friend holds several records as the World Kettlebell and the U.S. Kettlebell champion as well as in Kung Fu. His travel schedule for me was dependent on upcoming sessions with his trainers, one in Siberia, and one near his residence in the U.S. That was the breaking point for me personally, and I have hired my own trainer to keep me accountable towards a 12-week goal of mine. The personal accountability is pushing me towards my goal far more rapidly than venturing on my own or with someone less knowledgeable in this area of fitness. Please hire a professional at least twice/year to ensure you reset your body weight "set point" and fitness levels.

Remember that it will take 6-12 months to maintain your new body weight in order to permanently reset your body weight set point. All too often, I have witnessed someone lose the excess fat, reach their goal, and then believe that it is ok to have a few cocktails, pizza, fast food, etc. several times each week. They rapidly blow back up to their nemesis body weight set point. It's even worse when he brings his little sister "5 pounds extra" with him. You will lose an astonishing amount of excess body fat significantly and consistently by applying the permanent behavior strategies listed above.

Please go to http://www.upstatebootcamp.com/testimonials_ upstate_boot_camp.php to see before/after pictures of my clients' amazing transformations.

I am very happy you have decided to "Get with the Program." Please take the information I have shared and reclaim YOUR body, YOUR health, and YOUR closet!

About Pamela

Pamela Altstatt is the owner/program director for Upstate Adventure Boot Camp in South Carolina. She has a Master's degree in Exercise Physiology and a Bachelor's degree in Exercise Science. She is also certified in Sports Nutrition, as a Food Psychology Coach, Youth Fitness Coach, Personal Trainer and numerous other fitness certifications. She lived in Los Angeles for 17 years and administered fitness assessments for the Los Angeles Lakers, the Los Angeles Sparks, the Los Angeles Ice Dogs, competitors for the Ultimate Fighting Championship, and the Los Angeles Fire Department. She continues to work for various major professional sports teams and athletes on a contractual basis.

In Los Angeles, she also worked as a Clinical Exercise Physiologist on weekends and per diem for the cardiac rehabilitation programs at leading hospitals within the Los Angeles area. She would design and implement individual and group programs for heart and lung transplantation patients, coronary valve repair/replacement, angioplasty, and coronary bypass graft patients to measurably increase their quality of life, their fitness abilities, and their independence.

She has seen a wide range of individuals struggle with the ability to reclaim their body, their health, and their closets as well as witness a deep desire to take their athleticism to new levels. Pamela has helped them to not only accomplish their goals, but to actually supersede their initial expectations exponentially in a very short period of time.

Pamela and her husband, Hamilton, have partnered together to open Carolina Family Fitness in Seneca, South Carolina in order to help local athletes, overweight, obese youth as well as their moms, dads, and grandparents to get strong, lean and healthy.

Contact information: www.UpstateBootCamp.com

Email: Coach@UpstateBootCamp.com

CHAPTER 14

THE CULTURE OF FOOD

BY RYAN PANG

Being born and raised in Hawaii (on the island of Oahu), food is embedded into our lives from the moment we are born. Every gathering, we have a plethora of pupus (Hawaiian word for appetizers). It is such a part of my life that for example, when my family who now lives on the mainland comes back to visit, their entire trip is planned around where they want to eat while they are here. Everything else is pretty much just to kill time till the next meal. It's not just unique to my family though, if you come for a visit and ask any local what you should do while you are visiting, I can promise you that at least a few, if not most, of the suggestions will be "You can't miss going to _____ and trying their _____" – something specific like malasads, shave ice, coco puffs or something the place is known for. It's just a part of our culture that much here on Oahu, and I'm sure in other places across the country too.

For as long as I can remember, any time I went to a friend or relatives house or if anyone ever came over to ours, no matter how short they planned to stay, food (usually dessert of some kind) and drinks were always brought out, and it was always insisted that we eat – sometimes to the point where you would feel it rude to decline. This is just something that is a way of life in Hawaii when it comes to hospitality.

So, as you can see, food has always been a very big part of my life (as I'm sure it is for most people) as well. This kind of culture, while being an amazing place to be raised, can really take a toll on your waistline. Trying to stay healthy amongst all of these temptations and traditions is very difficult and a real challenge that I face every day living here, and I'm sure that you can understand where I'm coming from as you probably have your weaknesses for certain foods that you just can't pass on. My love of food and passion for the fitness industry is really what drives me to love learning about nutrition, and being able to enjoy food while still being healthy. I mean who wants to have a diet that consists of grilled chicken breast and steamed vegetables for the rest of their lives? I believe food is meant to bring joy and happiness, and invokes great pleasure and fond memories, so why should you have to be torn between them and reaching your goals? This is why learning tips on how to stick to a healthy lifestyle and what a healthy diet even is, was extremely important – while still being able to enjoy the foods that I love. Part of the reason I got into this industry was to help as many people as I can and I want to share what I have learned.

First off, let's get down to the basics of a good diet. As most trainers will probably tell you, diet is 80% of your success. Where people get these numbers I have no clue, but the premise is something I truly believe in. Without having a good diet, getting to your fitness goals is going to be extremely difficult through exercise alone. If you are the exception and are able to eat whatever you want and still get to your goals… Well, just know the rest of us hate you for having such amazing genes. For the rest of us, here is what works.

Go through this list and check off any of these guidelines you already incorporate into your life. If the listed guideline is only a "sometimes", then it's something you still need to work on, so don't check that one off. Over time, the more of these you have checked off, the easier it will be to get the body you want.

THE GUIDELINES:

1. Write down everything you eat. Even if you know you're going to eat junk food.

Research shows that most people just don't have a good idea of what their food intake really looks like until they measure and record it.

2. No processed foods. This includes but is not limited to anything with flour and added refined sugar.

3. Drink plenty of water. Shoot to work up to at least half your body weight in ounces of water per day.

4. Have protein, fat and veggies at every meal.

5. Take a high quality fish oil, D3, and multi-vitamin supplement. This will help to make sure that you have enough vitamins and minerals to have your body function properly. Ideally, you should be getting enough from your whole food intake, but this is a 'just in case.' The safe upper limit of fish oil is 3g of Omega-3 and the upper limit for D3 is 4000 IU. In any case, I recommend that you get tested for these levels and/or have a doctor recommend a specific dosage.

6. Eliminate any liquid that had calories or is called "diet" anything. Let's be honest. You know that fake "sugars" with zero calories are not so good for you despite having zero calories. At the very least, cutting out of fake "sugars" can help curb sugar cravings.

Now you have a list (the ones that aren't checked off) of diet guidelines that need improvement, and we will work on them one at a time. The whole reason I suggest you take them on one at a time is to increase your chances of succeeding at incorporating that particular guideline into your habits. Try to do too many at once, and oftentimes you will have trouble succeeding.

Remember, this is a marathon, not a sprint. We aren't looking for the quick fix to look good next week. We are looking for a better life long-term and for this program to become part of your life, so you can still enjoy food that brings back fond memories and joy, but still work towards the fitness goal you have set for yourself – whether it's to look great in a bikini for summer or a vacation, fit into those jeans in the back of your closet again, or maintain your figure through all the parties and sweets over the holiday season.

So here is how the program works. I want you to track for two weeks how well you followed the guideline you chose to work on as well as the guidelines you already have checked off. That's all you track. Don't worry about the other ones or anything else regarding your diet. It'll all come together in the end. When you have gotten that guideline down for 90% of your meals, then you have succeeded in making it part of your diet arsenal. Check off that guideline and pick another one to work on for the next two weeks. If at two weeks, you weren't 90% compliant with that guideline, don't worry about it. Take a deep breath, remind yourself why your goal is important to you, then recommit to getting right back on track.

I've always loved building things or knowing how to take them apart and putting them back together. I guess I get that from both my grandfathers and my dad. Not seeing where I'm going with this?? I see my job as learning how the body works, how to build the best program to get a result, to take apart what you are doing now and tinker with what you love to do to help you get the body you want. And if you don't love working out, don't have time for it or just flat out hate exercise, trust me I can still help you get that body you want. Don't get me wrong, exercise is very important and will help you to get to your goals faster if you chose to go that route, but again, your diet is how the game is won or lost when it comes to getting the body you want.

If you have a similar love for food like I do (my TV is always on shows like Unique Eats, Top Chef, Unique Sweets, Eat St, and Diners, Drive-Ins and Dives), then you'll understand how difficult it can be to get the body you want while still satisfying that love of food. Here are some tips that might help you if you are having trouble sticking to the diet program.

Plan your splurge meals ahead of time if you know you have a family dinner, or are going out for drinks with friends where it will be very difficult to stick to your diet plan ahead. I don't mean pack a Ziploc bag of approved diet food and bring it with you to the restaurant (although you could do that if you want). What I mean is, knowing that on Friday I'm going out to a party, well then, that is one less splurge meal I can have throughout the week and still be 90% compliant with my plan. If you plan/mark your known splurge meals ahead of time, you'll be less likely to have too many in any given week.

When grocery shopping, keep in mind that in most cases if it's got an ingredient list, you probably shouldn't buy it and you typically want to shop the perimeter of the market. I have yet to find a market where the perishable healthy foods aren't along the perimeter. Don't tempt yourself by going down the aisles looking for groceries.

Don't test your will power. You will eventually give in. Make sure when you go shopping, a good rule of thumb is to shop the rim of the aisles. Meaning where you find all the perishable things are like meats, fruits, and vegetables. If it doesn't go bad or need to be refrigerated in a couple of days it's probably not good for you. Everything else in the aisles and things that have a log shelf life just don't even buy or bring into your house. If you don't have it conveniently in the house, then you'll have a better chance of not eating it. If you really are craving something that's not diet friendly, by all means take a splurge meal and go out and satisfy your craving. Just don't bring the leftovers home. This way your splurge meal stays at one meal and doesn't roll over into multiple splurges just because it's there calling your name. Get used to wasting food if it's not on the diet plan. It is very hard for me as well, but it's really what's best for your waist line.

Most of us have heard of essential amino acids (protein) and essential fat/fatty acids (fat), but none of us have ever heard of essential carbohydrates right? Why is that? It's because there aren't any. You would be surprised as to how few carbs your body actually needs to function and how much of your diet is actually from carbs. This isn't to say that I'm promoting a zero-carb diet. Fruits and vegetables are carbs. You just don't need to over-consume the other types like bread, pasta, rice, etc. Those types of carbs don't serve a purpose in your diet other than because you love eating them. If fiber is going to be your argument, just keep in mind that calorie-for-calorie, fruits and veggies have way more fiber than any whole-grain 'anything' and they fall into the category of nutrient dense but not calorie dense, which means you can eat a ton of it and not really worry about packing on the pounds. Whole grains are not the only good source of fiber, so try replacing those starchy carbs on your plate with more vegetables and protein and see what happens to you body.

You don't have to eat less to lose weight. You can usually just change what you are eating for better quality food. For example, increase the amount of protein and vegetables you eat. Odds are your diet is mostly carbohydrates and you could stand to add a bunch more veggies and a few more servings of protein. Why? Well because again, veggies are nutrient dense and not calorie dense so you can eat more (see, you don't have to eat less to lose weight), and the protein is because it burns inefficiently. What does that mean? It means that even though you eat protein, it's 4cal/g, that's not actually the end result when your body breaks it down. It's what we call the thermic effect of food. There is a lot of energy burned off in the breakdown process of protein (again you get to eat more and weigh less – win/win). In addition, starchier carbs tend to be very calorie dense making it very easy to over-consume them, so just on a volume basis, switching for protein or vegetables will drastically decrease your calorie consumption. Also, if you find yourself overeating or with a plate full of non-diet-friendly foods, try eating your veggies first.

Don't shoot for a perfect or ideal diet. Rather go with one that is practical and realistic for you. Practice makes progress and that's all we are looking for to help you improve week over week at eating well.

If you happen to have an unexpected splurge meal, don't get down on yourself and give up. If you had a flat tire you wouldn't just say 'screw it' and slash the other three, now would you? Just say "it's in the past and there is nothing I can do about it now," and get right back on track with your next meal. Remember that one bad meal does not make a person fat, just as one perfect meal does not make one skinny. It is the culmination (of your choices over time that will determine if you will have success or not with your diet). It is the choices you make over time that will determine the effects of those good or bad decisions.

If you know you are going to have a splurge meal, (hopefully you do because you are planning these out), consider drinking a giant glass of water about 15-20 min before you sit down to eat. This will help you put some no-calories volume (see the theme going on here?) in your stomach and at an early enough time that your stomach has time to communicate with your brain telling it the stomach is partially filled. This will allow you to enjoy your splurge meal but also help to control the quantity you can pack away in that given time frame, so even if you consume until you are bursting at the seams, you have still eaten/drank less than you would have fit into your stomach, because you drank that water.

"A journey of a thousand miles begins with a single step"
~ Lao-tzu

Feeling hesitant that this diet program is for you? Just focus on taking that first step. I mean, what's the worst that will happen? The worst case is that nothing changes and you ate healthy for a couple of weeks or months. Best case is you've changed your life and taken a big leap forward towards the body you've always wanted, so why not just give it your best shot and see what happens.

About Ryan

Growing up, Ryan Pang was very active in sports like baseball, soccer, and volleyball. He had been drawn to the fitness industry ever since being introduced to the weight room in his sophomore year in high school and continues to do so to this day – turning his hobby and passion into a career of helping others.

Ryan Pang graduated with a degree in Exercise Science and a minor in Business in 2007. Shortly after graduating, he received his American Council on Exercise personal training certification. Committed to educational excellence, Ryan continued to receive multiple certifications including the National Academy of Sports Medicine personal training, Suspension Training & Group Suspension Training, Functional Movement Screen, and the prestigious Precision Nutrition certification.

In 2009, Ryan started Fitness HI, whose goal is to provide the highest level of service to his select clients. He recently opened Hawaii's premier (fitness, fat loss,) studio in heart of Honolulu in order to help people reach their fitness goals.

Committed to providing his clientele with the best and most advanced fat loss results, Ryan is a member of several industry-leading mastermind groups as well as regularly attending seminars held by some of the top fitness professionals in the world, like *Men's Health* top 10 gym in the country, Results Fitness. It is through this participation that Ryan is sought after for his expertise in fitness and nutritional coaching.

For more information on Ryan and Fitness HI or how you too can realize your fitness potential:

Visit: www.FitnessHI.com
Or email him at: Ryan@FitnessHI.com
You can also check Fitness HI out on Facebook and Twitter.

CHAPTER 15

"FORE" THE LOVE OF THE GAME
— Your Executive Golfer

BY PETER LEVIDIS

Your mission should you choose to accept it: Hit that diminutive white dimpled ball 275 yards in the direction of the hole with the flag in it! No small feat.

It has only been in the past couple of decades that fitness and golf can be mentioned in the same sentence. Fitness has always played a role, but the typical bodybuilding, biceps-growing and seated rotation-back-pain-inducing-machines dominated the scene. Exercises were machine-based and seated working only one plane of movement at a time. Posture and flexibility were an after- thought. "What do you mean I have to stretch my lats? What lats?"

As Athletic Therapists, we were constantly rehabilitating golfers who were experiencing chronic recurring injuries due mainly to poor swing mechanics and less-than-ideal posture. Golfer's elbows, rotator cuff issues, sciatic pains, bursitis in the hips, were some of the more common ailments. Their body was simply not moving as efficiently as it should, creating overuse strain at various joints.

Melanie, my wife and business partner, and I, recognized the need to bridge the gap between rehabilitating their injuries and improving their overall body mechanics to prevent the reoccurrence as well as improve their performance. After all, statistics show that over 50% of golfers are playing with some degree of pain or injury.

It is paramount to identify the source of the problem and not just focus on the painful joint. For example, a restriction in thoracic mobility will limit the golfer's rotation; to compensate, he/she has to increase the work of the arms to generate power through the swing, causing increase stress on the elbows and bringing about the dreaded elbow tendinitis. Until the thoracic mobility and posture are improved, the golfer will continue to suffer from this condition while playing.

THEIR NEEDS AND WANTS

Your executive golfer W*ANTS* the following:

1. Longer drives

2. Lower scores

Your executive golfer *NEEDS* the following:

1. More mobility in the ankle, hip, upper back, shoulder and neck

2. More stability in the foot, knee, lower back, and shoulder blade (scapula)

Golfers are always looking for that "extra edge" that will bring them closer to a better golf game. Their bodies are the extra edge they are looking for. The golfer needs to optimize their standing posture, transfer weight from side to side, produce explosive rotation and be able to decelerate rotation. Prescribing a personalized training program that will improve these elements will decrease the likelihood of overuse injuries and lower their handicap. Every golfer knows exactly what a golf swing should look like. However, they are limited by their physical restrictions.

"We don't believe there is one way to swing a club; we believe there are an infinite number of ways to swing a club. But we do believe that there is one efficient way for all golfers to swing a club and it is based on what they can physically do."
~Titleist

Technology plays a role, no doubt. The money spent on this sport in Research and Development is remarkable! Newly improved golf balls and club fittings are crucial to a golfer's performance. However, his/her body still remains the ultimate investment. As the golfer ages, flexibility will decrease, strength and power will diminish, and thus the likelihood of chronic injuries increases and golf handicaps surge. A sound golf fitness assessment and program will strengthen weaknesses and build upon his/her strengths. Unfortunately golf is still often thought of as a game, not as a sport. Driving a golf ball is a highly athletic movement. Average club head speed with a driver is often over 100mph and amateur golfers recruit 90% of their peak muscle activity when driving a ball. Yet many still refuse to include conditioning as part of their preparation to play golf!

Paul, one of our executive golfers mentions, "I was in the best golf shape when I was in my 20's…I was a 7 handicap. However, with work and family commitments, golf took a back seat." Medical and orthopaedic concerns started to plague Paul, which hampered his efforts to remain active with golf. His posture deteriorated. He presented with forward head posture, tight pectoral muscles, weak lower abs and tight hamstrings. Shoulder mobility was reduced, limiting external rotation, due to the stiffness in the upper back and previous injuries. Hip restrictions caused by long hours spent sitting behind a desk resulting in chronically tight hip flexors. This is not uncommon for golfers as they age.

STARTING OUT:

Whether the golfer has no previous training history, is a weekend warrior or a seasoned athlete, the testing must be standardized and individual. This will allow for customization of their program, as no two people are the same. "If you don't test, it is just a guess," says Titleist. The following protocol is what we use in our studio to prepare the golfer physically:

1. Full body standing postural scan (front, back and both side views).

2. Full body extremity scan complete with range of motion (ROM) and resisted isometric (RISO) testing.

3. Evaluation using the K-Trainer (k-trainer.com): 3D wireless software that projects their computerized image onto the screen. It allows us to objectively record the golfer's ability to rotate symmetrically, transfer weight and dissociate upper and lower body.

4. Functional Movement Screen (FMS) screen – which is a grading system designed to assess movement.

5. Discussion with their golf pro as to what physical limitations are being encountered and what steps are being taken to progress.

The following characteristics are necessary for a golfer to have regardless of age. Mastering these seven important elements will improve the golfers' performance with the least risk of injury.

1. Proper hip hinge mechanics

2. Proper alignment of the cervical, thoracic, and lumbar spine

3. Stability to be able to transfer weight from side to side

4. Symmetrical rotation of the trunk

5. Strength throughout the swing

6. Power development upon impact

7. No loss of posture THROUGHOUT the golf swing

Now that we have assessed our golfer and understand their physical strengths and weaknesses as well as the movements required for them, we can now design their customized program. The following is the golf fitness template that we use at The S.P.O.R.T. Specialists Inc.:

RAMP (Range of Motion, Activation, Movement Preparation)

R= foam rolling, ball massaging, stretching tight muscles

A= waking up muscles that have been ignored or inhibited by the tight ones

MP= preparing and alerting the body for ACTION through golf specific drills

We do not "warm up" our golfers anymore. Walking on a treadmill or biking for a few minutes prior to beginning an exercise routine is doing nothing to "prepare" the person and actually may even be counterproductive. We RAMP them up as is being taught throughout the industry by fitness leaders, Alwyn and Rachel Cosgrove at Results Fitness. This RAMP helps to restore better mobility and awakens the nervous system, which prepares them for their program and the repetitive and explosive demands of the golf swing.

Core training:
The buzzword nowadays is that everyone should work the core.

"I'm doing 100 crunches daily in the morning…it's my core exercise for the day!"

Golf requires upper and lower body synergy, and what links them together is the core musculature of the trunk. Working in isolation, i.e., crunches, does not train this and can actually be detrimental. Core training exercises should strengthen this link and combine movements that can mimic the golf swing and its multiple planes of motion. A great example of this would be a Standing Woodchop. It involves lateral weight transfer, posture control, rotation of the upper torso and shoulders and pelvic stability. The core muscles are responsible for keeping the upper and lower body synched.

Power:
Power conditioning comes next. Our golfers, young or old, MUST swing the golf club with some degree of power when they play. Therefore, excluding power exercises in an exercise program will never allow for a proper carry-over. Lower body power exercises are JUST as important as upper body rotary exercises. The medicine ball side toss onto a wall is a perfect example: stand in a golf stance; toss the medicine ball laterally towards a wall following through all the way.

Strength Circuits:
The strength and conditioning is the portion of our program design template that will incorporate functional multi-joint movement exercises to allow for better carry-over to the golfer. The exercises should NOT mimic the golf swing exactly but train the movements, broken down, that are necessary in the golf swing. The golfer MUST do strengthening exercises that will incorporate the following elements:

1. Exercises that are done standing NOT sitting

2. Movements that train the disassociation of upper and lower body

3. Exercises that incorporate all three planes of movement

4. Exercises that will train balance and coordination

Paul's routine:

Paul had cardiac problems as well as lower back surgery creating more roadblocks. "At one point I was on crutches because my back was hurting so much and was incapable of functioning properly. I was down to playing anywhere between 3-5 rounds of golf for the year!" he says. When Paul first started with our "Golf Performance Program," there was resistance in that the majority of movement that we asked him to perform created some degree of discomfort and soreness for a few days thereafter. He believed in the process and persisted with his training religiously.

This is where our background in Athletic Therapy kicked in. Along with movement specific drills, it was necessary for Paul to get some manual work done to improve his body's abilities to move. Stretching alone was not cutting it.

– Manual work to improve the mobility of his joints, namely the thoracic spine, shoulders and shoulder blades and hips.

– Corrective postural exercises at work and at home (office desk setup, proper sleeping positions, etc.).

– Increase in water intake and better nutrition to improve muscle function and total body well being.

– Releasing tension on scars from surgeries.

All of this was necessary to allow him to "Get With The Program." Paul realized that his health and fitness came first and golf was secondary. "I want to be able to enjoy the sport of golf, and it was an eye opener for me to actually join a gym. I am not yet where I would like to be. I would still like to get even better and fitter for my age so that I can enjoy golf for as long as I can."

His posture, weight transfer, hip flexors, lat muscles, hips, thoracic spine ALL needed to be addressed and are still a staple in his exercise diet. With the simplest of exercises providing an "opening up" effect, to more complicated balancing exercises, Paul has achieved a healthier attitude and appreciation towards how golf fitness can help improve all performance attributes. After all, it's "fore" the love of the game!

He has been with us for almost a year and has decreased his back pain substantially and has improved his standing posture. While down south this winter, he was able to play 5 rounds of golf in 5 consecutive days: a great achievement! Now that the snow has melted, he is looking forward to playing golf more consistently and frequently this summer. In addition, Paul recently mentioned to us that he had his best round of golf in about ten years.

Tracking his progress was crucial. We were able to monitor all improvements in his flexibility, stability, strength and power. This allowed us to modify the routine when needed.

We have noted the following improvements in his physical being:

1. Paul is able to rotate his thoracic spine with very little restrictions in his shoulders.

2. The increase in his thoracic mobility led to better neck mobility.

3. He is standing up taller than ever before and usually even taller when he completes his program.

4. He can effectively rotate his pelvis from his trunk.

5. Strength in his core by holding different planks for up to 45 seconds with excellent form.

6. Balance on a stability disc on one foot with little support.

PAUL'S INITIAL PROGRAM

Following the protocol we outlined in this chapter, ANY level of golfer can make dramatic improvements in their capacity to play a more efficient game of golf, with the least amount of risk of injury. He/she must understand that golf is not a game but a sport, which involves athleticism, coordination, flexibility, strength and power. The following is a synopsis of what is needed for any golfer:

1. A proper and thorough assessment (physical testing of posture, joints, and movement patterns).

2. Develop a thorough golf-specific training program that addresses weaknesses and instabilities.

3. Track the progress.

4. Discuss with his/her golf pro.

5. Constant fine-tuning of the program to ensure continued progress.

About Peter

Peter Levidis, B.Sc., CAT(C)

Peter holds a Bachelor of Science degree from Concordia University in Montreal. He received his certification as a Strength & Conditioning Specialist and as an Athletic Therapist in 1996 and 1997, respectively. To get a more profound understanding of sports performance, Peter received accreditation from the CHEK institute as a Golf Biomechanics Specialist and a CHEK level 2 Practitioner.

Since 2000, Peter has co-owned The S.P.O.R.T. Specialists Inc. with his wife, Melanie Scrase. Both Peter and Melanie continually update their knowledge and communicate that to their clientele, a client base ranging from weekend warriors to amateurs and professionals from all sports.

Peter has had the honour of being part of the pre-season and post-season physical testing for the Montreal Canadiens and their farm team, the Hamilton Bulldogs, and has successfully developed dry-land training programs for Midget AAA hockey teams, elite swimmers, water-polo, runners and triathletes. A highlight of his career was when he was hired to work as the Athletic Therapist and Strength Coach for the Canadian Star Boat Sailing Team for the 2013 Olympics in London.

Working closely with local golf pros in the area, Peter has been sought after to help with the strength and conditioning for young, up-and-coming golfers as young as 12 years old. Peter thrives on seeing to what potential he can get a golfer to play. His attention to detail and ability to identify the slightest imbalances allow Peter to perfect his golfers' abilities.

He has lectured at major companies, universities, sports teams, communities, and to allied health practitioners. His scientific and logical approach to fitness and conditioning has been the focus of numerous television spots, newspaper articles, and radio spots. He continues to travel and learn, attending workshops from the best names in the business, to have his studio stand out in the crowd of gyms.

For more information on Peter Levidis and The S.P.O.R.T. Specialists Inc., visit:
www.sportspecialists.ca

The S.P.O.R.T. Specialists Inc.
Dorval, Montreal, Quebec
(514) 556-4994